*Family Traditions That
Last a Lifetime*

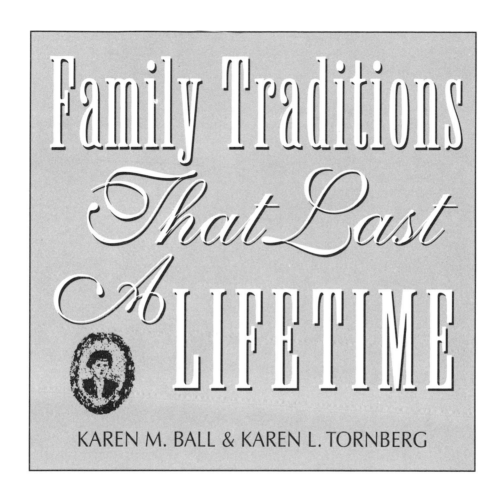

Family Traditions That Last A LIFETIME

KAREN M. BALL & KAREN L. TORNBERG

Tyndale House Publishers, Inc. Wheaton, Illinois

Library of Congress Cataloging-in-Publication Data

Ball, Karen, date
    Family traditions that last a lifetime / Karen M. Ball and Karen
L. Tornberg.
        p.   cm.
    ISBN 0-8423-1371-0
    1. Family festivals—United States—Quotations, maxims, etc.
2. Family—United States—Religious life—Quotations, maxims, etc.
3. United States—Social life and customs—Quotations, maxims, etc.
I. Tornberg, Karen L.   II. Title.
GT2402.U6B34   1993
390—dc20   93-7547

Printed in the United States of America

99 98 97 96 95 94 93
9   8   7   6   5   4   3   2

What people are saying about *Family Traditions That Last a Lifetime*

"Family Traditions lovingly helps define who we are and what makes us family. We all need ideas, inspiration on how to encourage the family unit. In these stress-filled days, we need 'family' more than ever. This book helps!"

BILL AND NANCIE CARMICHAEL
publishers
Virtue and *Christian Parenting* magazines

"Here's a *very practical* tool for building dimension into your family life—a tool that is as fun-filled as it is faith filled!"

JACK W. HAYFORD
senior pastor
The Church on the Way

"I love this book! It is both fun and serious. Nothing is more important than learning to enrich our lives with others—and this book shows how to do that in a unique fashion. Some books should be read from cover to cover. This one needs to be sampled all year long!"

GILBERT MORRIS
author

"In my work over the last two decades with America's youth, I am convinced that the stronghold of Christian values is made in the home. I consider family memory-making the most valuable and rewarding thing I am called to do."

JOE WHITE, ED.D.
president
Kanakuk-Kanakomo Kamps, Inc.

"I am overcome with admiration for this book! It is filled to the full with wonderful ideas . . . its practical spiritual insights are profound. I am sending copies to my ten children because of the help and blessing it will be to their families and to my twenty-eight grandchildren. And my grandchildren in turn will pass along these traditions to their children in the years ahead!

"This book is a treasure chest, full of joys for your family now, and for your extended family and for your friends."

KENNETH N. TAYLOR
translator of *The Living Bible*

Some of the people whose thoughts and ideas you'll find in this book . . .

Abigail Adams
Ann Kiemel Anderson
Pat Baker
Ron Ball
Timothy Botts
Jeff and Beau Bridges
Christie Brinkley
Dr. Joyce Brothers
Carol Burnett
Leo F. Buscaglia
Barbara Bush
Bill and Nancie Carmichael
Steven and Lisa (Whelchel) Cauble
Rick Christian
Winston Churchill
Robert Cook
Denton A. Cooley
Bill Cosby
Donna Fletcher Crow
Charles Dickens
Shirley Dobson
T. S. Eliot
Ted Engstrom
Anne Frank
Annette Funicello
Kenneth Gangel
Billy Graham
Amy Grant
Rosey Greer
Randy Harper
Irene Burk Harrell
Jack Hayford
Charles and Bari Hill
Lou Holtz
Mary Ruth Howes
Gary and Angela Hunt
Dave and Neta Jackson

Thomas Jefferson
Jerry and Dianna Jenkins
Mark and Debbie Jevert
John Paul II
Lady Bird Johnson
John Henry Jowett
Naomi Judd
Evie Tornquist Karlsson
Grace Kelly
Rose Kennedy
Graham Kerr
Jay Kesler
Grace Ketterman
Martin Luther King, Jr.
Madeleine L'Engle
Tim and Beverly LaHaye
Tom Landry
Marlene LeFever
Eda Leshan
C. S. Lewis
Paul Lewis
Abraham Lincoln
Art Linkletter
Florence Littauer
Henry Wadsworth Longfellow
Martin Luther
George Macdonald
Judith Martin
Martin E. Marty
Josh and Dottie McDowell
Bob and Ann McGrath
Margaret Mead
Frank B. Minirth
D. L. Moody
Harold Myra
Ogden Nash
Don Osgood

Christian Overman
Louis Pasteur
Sandi Patti
Walter Payton
Marilyn Quayle
Nancy Reagan
Ronald Reagan
Willard Scott
William Shakespeare
Dinah Shore
Mike Singletary
Ricky Skaggs
Lewis Smedes
Jerry Spinelli
Tim Stafford
Eda Stertz
Noel Paul Stookey
Chuck Swindoll
Corrie ten Boom
Mother Teresa
John Tesh
Ingrid Trobisch
Mark Twain
Queen Victoria
Meredith Vieira
Shirley Pope Waite
Sheila Walsh
Walter Wangerin, Jr.
Jim Watkins
Paul Welter
Joan E. White
Joe White
Thomas B. White
David Wilkerson
D. Charles Williams
Deneice Williams
Woodrow Wilson

Heartfelt thanks to all who shared their memories and traditions with us!
Karen M. Ball and Karen L. Tornberg.

To my family—God knew what he was doing when he put us together. I love you!

KMB

To Mom, Dad, and Mark—with much love and many thanks. And to Judy—the closest I'll ever come to having a sister.

KLT

Contents

Foreword

I am overcome with admiration for this book! It is filled to the full with wonderful ideas about achieving family togetherness. Its practical spiritual insights are profound.

I wish this book had been around when my children were at home. What a wealth of great thoughts would have been available to give our family extra joy. We had our happy traditions, but here are hundreds of others to choose from that hadn't occurred to me then. And even now, with the nest empty, I've come across some excellent ideas for just the two of us.

Obviously I am sending copies to my ten children because of the help and blessing it will be to their families and to my twenty-eight grandchildren. And my grandchildren in turn will pass along these traditions to their children in the years ahead!

So this book is a treasure chest, full of joys for your family now, and for your extended family and for your friends.

May there be ever-increasing joy in your home. This book will bless you and yours.

KENNETH N. TAYLOR
Founder and Chairman of the Board,
Tyndale House Publishers
Translator, The Living Bible

Preface

The family is one of nature's masterpieces.
George Santayana

I like being with people. In fact, I thrive on it! There is nothing so warm and safe as the sense of belonging I get from being with someone who loves me. And there is no sense of belonging so wonderful as the one I get from being with my family.

It is fascinating to me that immediately after having created man, God's reaction was, "It is not good for the man to be alone" (Gen. 2:18). If there was an "owner's manual" for humans, I have a feeling God's remark would be one of the primary cautions: "Do not allow this model to operate alone." There seems to be plenty of evidence in the Bible that we need others: "Where two or three are gathered in my name," "Two are better than one," "God sets the lonely in families," and so on. I like to think that is one reason God gave us the family. He knew that if we were left on our own, we'd probably only get into trouble and make ourselves miserable. So he placed us with others, to learn, to grow, to discover together what it means to be human, to be ourselves, to be part of something. He gave us our earthly families so that we might gain a brief glimpse into what it will be when we are together with him, our heavenly Father, the founder of our kingdom family.

Most people would agree that a family is a good thing. And while our individual families may not always be what we want them to be, they still are a rich source of growth, pride, laughter, wisdom, faith, embarrassment, humility . . . of all that there is to experience in life.

I think I have the best family that ever existed. My mom and dad and my two brothers aren't perfect—but they are mine, and they love me. I wouldn't give them up for anything (not even my brothers!). That's why I wanted to do this book, to somehow remind myself—and you—that in the midst of a hurting and hurtful world our families are a wondrous gift. There is much joy to be found in our families. We need to find ways to cherish and nurture each other, to recognize what we have. It is my hope that the traditions, ideas, and quotes you find in these pages will help you do just that.

As you read, I hope God will bring you many moments of laughter, insight, and enjoyment. And I hope, above all, that you will gain a new appreciation of what you have in your own family.

KAREN M. BALL

*F*or me the word *family* takes on many meanings.

Being single, I have no husband or children (yet) to call my immediate family. So when I think of family, my thoughts begin, naturally, with my parents and brother. They are a source of strength and comfort, love and laughter without which my existence would be greatly diminished.

My extended family is small: an aunt, uncle, two cousins and their families. We are lucky to live close together so we can celebrate holidays gathered as a family. These times together give me a sense of belonging and continuity.

I have friends who live nearby whom I consider family.

And they have told me I am a part of theirs in that special way people can "adopt" people they love.

My first job was in a small office—we referred to ourselves as family, and in many ways we were. I have been blessed with many dear friends who are like sisters and brothers. My best friend's children call me "Aunt Karen." I like the sound of that.

Most recently I was asked to be a godmother to the son of college friends, so now there is even a child in my life without changing one diaper!

Summing it up, I have a rather large—if greatly extended—family! To each one I offer my love and thanks for filling out my family tree.

May your family be as diverse and supportive, no matter how you define it!

KAREN L. TORNBERG

How to Use This Book

The mere fact that you have picked up this book indicates you have an interest in the preservation and strengthening of your family. Now, where do you go from here?

Included in this volume are traditions used by people from every walk of life as well as some practical ideas for new traditions (or at least they are new to us!). Find the ones you like. Use them as they are or adapt them to fit your own family.

Use the Table of Contents if you are looking for a particular type of tradition to fit a specific time of year, holiday, or other occasion. Or just begin browsing from the beginning and mark the traditions you would like to "adopt."

Since we are talking about the *family,* you may want to include family members in this process. Perhaps one of you will read the entire book and pick out ideas that are possibilities. Then gather everyone together and discuss which traditions sound best and vote on which ones you want to try.

The more personalized you can make these traditions, the more meaningful and fun they will be—and the more likely they are to become actual traditions in the sense that they are carried on year after year and passed down from generation to generation.

CHAPTER ONE

The Importance of Family

It is not good for the man to be alone.

GENESIS 2:18

Two are better than one. . . . If one falls down, his friend
can help him up. . . . Though one may be overpowered,
two can defend themselves. A cord of three strands
is not quickly broken.

ECCLESIASTES 4:9-10, 12

Every effort to make society sensitive to the importance of the
family is a great service to humanity.

POPE JOHN PAUL II

*K*ing Solomon conscripted laborers from all Israel—thirty thousand men. He sent them off to Lebanon in shifts of ten thousand a month, so that they spent one month in Lebanon and two months at home" (1 KINGS 5:13-14). ✤ Even in his time, King Solomon knew the value of the family unit to society as a whole. The following is the note in the *Life Application Bible* regarding this verse: "Solomon drafted three times the number of workers needed for the temple project and then arranged their schedules so they didn't have to be away from home for long periods of time. This showed his concern for the welfare of his workers and the importance he placed on family life. The strength of a nation is in direct proportion to the strength of its families. Solomon wisely recognized that family should always be a top priority" (LIFE APPLICATION BIBLE, NEW INTERNATIONAL VERSION, TYNDALE HOUSE PUBLISHERS, 555). ✤ Following is a collection of thoughts reminding us of the undeniable importance—to us as individuals, Christians, and a society—of developing strong values within the family unit. ~KLT

Apart from religious influence, the family is the most important unit of society. It would be well if every home were Christian, but we know that is not so. . . . The only way to provide the right home for your children is to put the Lord above them, and fully instruct them in the ways of the Lord. You are responsible before God for the home you provide for them.

BILLY GRAHAM
Evangelist and author

If this band has a message, it's urging moms and dads to stay together no matter how hard it gets, not just for the kids' sake, but for the sake of generations we'll never see.

RANDY HARPER
Keyboardist for Kentucky Thunder
(Ricky Skaggs' band) and
former church music minister

People are blind to what they really need. They need family, and they need religion. Period. There is such an incredible strength in family, and religion gives you respectability, responsibility, and a reverence for life.

WILLARD SCOTT
Television personality

Civilization varies with the family, and the family with civilization. Its highest and most complete realization is found where enlightened Christianity prevails; where woman is exalted to her true and lofty place as equal with the man; where husband and wife are one in honor, influence, and affection, and where children are a common bond of care and love. This is the idea of a perfect family.

WILLIAM AIKMAN

Call it a clan, call it a network, call it a tribe, call it a family. Whatever you call it, whoever you are, you need one.

JANE HOWARD

The family was ordained of God that children might be trained up for himself; it was before the church, or rather the first form of the church on earth.

POPE LEO XIII

Many parents do nothing about their children's religious education, telling them they can decide what they believe when they're twenty-one. That's like telling them they can decide when they're twenty-one whether or not they should brush their teeth. By then, their teeth may have fallen out. Likewise, their principles and morality may also be nonexistent.
                                        GRACE KELLY
                              Actress and Princess of Monaco

The family is more sacred than the state, and men are begotten not for the earth and for time, but for Heaven and eternity.
                                        POPE PIUS XI,
                                        Casti Connubii

Our generation's social revolution taught us that family life needs protection. Our laws, policies and society as a whole must support our families. Our generation has benefited as no other from the opportunities that America provides, so now is not the time to turn away from the values that brought us here. . . .
                                        MARILYN QUAYLE
                              Attorney and wife of former
                              vice president Dan Quayle

In 1965 the average parent spent thirty hours a week with a child. Today the average parent spends only seventeen hours.
                              FOCUS ON THE FAMILY BULLETIN

When **Mother Teresa** received her Nobel Prize she was asked, "What can we do to help promote world peace?" "Go home and love your family," she replied.

The family was established long before the church. My duty is to my family first.
                                        D. L. MOODY
                                        Evangelist

Families struggle to maintain adequate communication and togetherness. It seems our busy lives conspire to strangle the unity on which healthy families thrive. How essential, then, to elevate our family relationships to a higher priority. Give yourself to something that lasts—your family.

DR. KENNETH GANGEL
Dallas Seminary

No matter how many communes anybody invents, the family always creeps back.

MARGARET MEAD
Anthropologist

The family is the nucleus of civilization.

WILL AND ARIEL DURANT
Authors and historians

❖ In an interview with Sharon Donohue of *Today's Christian Woman* magazine, **Madeleine L'Engle** discussed her feelings about the importance of mothers being at home.

"If it is at all possible, I think women should stay at home with their children until they are in school. I think that's very important. But I also understand that for some women, it's just not financially feasible.

"I think those early years with the mother and father are the time for setting the children's understanding of God and the universe. When my children were little, prayer time was a long procedure of reading stories, singing songs, talking about God, and praying together. I suspect many working women are too tired for that by the end of the day."

Strong families are the foundation of society. Through them we pass on our traditions, rituals, and values. From them we receive the love, encouragement, and education needed to meet human challenges.

RONALD REAGAN
Actor and fortieth U.S. president

It [tradition] cannot be inherited, and if you want it you must obtain it by great labor.

T. S. ELIOT
Tradition and the Individual Talent

'Mid pleasures and palaces though we may roam,
Be it ever so humble, there's no place like home.

JOHN HOWARD PAYNE
Actor and American diplomat

FAMILY

The family is a little book,
The children are the leaves,
The parents are the cover that
Safe protection gives.
At first, the pages of the book
Are blank, and smooth, and fair;
But time soon writeth memories,
And painteth pictures there.
Love is the golden clasp
That bindeth up the trust;
O break it not, lest all the leaves
Shall scatter like the dust.   ANONYMOUS

Everything I know about history, every bit of experience and observation that has contributed to my thought, has confirmed me in the conviction that the real wisdom of human life is compounded out of the experiences of ordinary men.

WOODROW WILSON
Twenty-eighth U.S. president

What is the difference between a home and a house? Anybody can build a house; we need something more for the creation of a home. A house is an accumulation of brick and stone, with an assorted collection of manufactured goods; a home is the abiding place of ardent affection, of fervent hope, of genial trust.

There is many a homeless man who lives in a richly furnished house. There is many a modest house in the crowded street which is an illuminated and beautiful home. The sumptuously furnished house may be only an exquisitely sculptured tomb; the scantily furnished house may be the very hearthstone of the eternal God.

The Bible does not say very much about homes; it says a great deal about the things that make them.

It speaks about life and love and joy and peace and rest! If we get a house and put these into it, we shall have secured a home.

JOHN HENRY JOWETT

CHAPTER TWO

Family Traditions for Festivals

Go and enjoy choice food and sweet drinks, and send
some to those who have nothing prepared.
This day is sacred to our Lord.

NEHEMIAH 8:10

The life without festival is a long road without an inn.

DEMOCRITUS OF ABDERA

*O*ne of the things we did best in our house when I was growing up was celebrate together. Holidays, birthdays, anniversaries . . . they all were events. Every holiday was an opportunity for Mom and Dad to do something fun and imaginative, to remind us that we were special—and they never let us down. My mom was the undisputed queen of the holidays. She was a master at creating an atmosphere of celebration, always decorating the home for us and the basement for church gatherings, fixing just-right meals or treats, giving little gifts or signs that today was something to be enjoyed. My dad was the king of humor and ingenuity, always coming up with something funny or unusual to add to the festivities. I've included some of our family celebrations in the following section. In addition, you will find many other wonderful traditions and ideas to share with your family. I only pray that these times of celebration can become as precious to you and your children as they still are to me, and that you will use them as opportunities to share together in the life and love God has given us. ~KMB

New Year's Day

Make an annual list of the characteristics of a great family. Then individually rate your family and talk about your ratings. (For example, ten could be excellent; five, average; and one, awful.) Encourage each other to share ways to raise low ratings. Be careful that this doesn't become a time of preaching at or correcting the children. Instead, let it be a time of listening and growth.

Another idea is to write a family prayer together each year. Follow this PRAY pattern: **P**raise—Begin with a line of praise for what God has done for the family; **R**epentance—Pray that God will forgive sins in family members' lives; **A**sk—Ask Jesus to meet the needs of special friends outside the family; **Y**ou: Ask Jesus for things your family would like him to do for you. Then read that prayer several times during the year.

MARLENE LEFEVER
Author and church curriculum specialist

Every New Year's Day, our family gets together and chooses a new hobby to take on. So far we've enjoyed bird watching, photography, camping, swimming lessons, painting, and building birdhouses. It gives us something special to do as a family every year.

MARGARET SANDERS

We live on a farm and enjoy taking long walks in the country. On the last day of 1991 the children and I took a walk. We talked about all the new or eventful things that had happened that year, and then we looked at how God's hand had been in those events. Then we stated what we might want to take place in 1992 and prayed, as we walked, for God to be with us each day during all events of the upcoming year.

My children are three, five, and six years old and still learning how God works. This was a great teaching time for me to relay the wonders of our Lord and his magnificent presence in our lives. And what a meaningful way to close a year and enter a new one.

This is a new "tradition" that I'm sure will be repeated for years to come!

DAWN ROBERTS

Every year, when the new calendars come out in the stores, I pick up a special one just for me and my wife. I circle one day a month in red, then write on the cover 'Red-letter days are our days together.' This way we know we have at least one day a month when we can be just the two of us, doing something we enjoy.

TOM OWENS

In our home in Haarlem, Holland, Father used to read Psalm 91 from the Bible and pray the very moment the first of January began. We consciously went into the new year together with the Lord.

CORRIE TEN BOOM
Evangelist and author

He who dwells in the shelter of the Most High
will rest in the shadow of the Almighty.
I will say of the Lord, "He is my refuge and my fortress,
my God, in whom I trust." **PSALM 91:1-2**

Every once in a while, it's nice to get a good shot of romance and . . . well, magic. For us, that time is New Year's Eve, when we throw a huge party for all of our neighbors and special friends.

Invitations arrive at homes on December 1, before people have generally made plans. We ask for an RSVP by December 10, which allows us to send a second round of invitations if it doesn't look like the house will be filled.

To set the mood, we string thousands of little white lights (available at half-price after Christmas) *everywhere* throughout the house: around windows and entryways, along the top of kitchen cabinets and countertops, interwoven in garlands draped on the hearth and banisters, etc. These lights are supplemented by dozens of silver garlands (again, sales galore after Dec. 25) and silver helium-filled balloons tied with silver ribbons (check rental stores for helium tanks and party suppliers for balloons). Once the house is decorated and the lights are lit, it truly looks like a magical wonderland. A little music, lots of food and beverages, and a houseful of people—these are the rest of the ingredients for a great kickoff for the new year. If you want to go all out, make it a black-tie optional affair (many people love an excuse to really dress up), and invite a musician or small group to play for a couple of hours (check yellow pages or ask school/church music leaders for contacts).

As midnight nears, we pass out stupid hats and noisemakers and, at the stroke of twelve, everybody sings "Auld Lang Syne." What can I say, but it beats sitting around the TV watching other people celebrate in Times Square! THE FAMILY OF RICK CHRISTIAN
Author and publishing agent

Valentine's Day

Valentine's Day has become a focal point for Scripture memory at our house. We use Valentine's Day to work on trying to hide God's Word in our hearts. Each person chooses a verse to memorize during the day, then shares it at our evening meal. BRENDA POINSETT
Author

❖ Start your spouse's day off right. Put a fresh flower with a ribbon tied around it on the seat of his or her car. If possible, sneak the flower into the car early that morning so that it will be there to greet your spouse when he or she opens the car. Also, tape a note of love and encouragement to the steering wheel. Tell your spouse at least one specific thing that you enjoy and appreciate about him or her.

A big green box was the container of old valentines, lace ribbons, and trimmings of all kinds. In early February, we used these contents to make the valentines we gave away. Each one was a creative, individual "masterpiece," which clearly communicated our love for our friends. GRACE H. KETTERMAN, M.D.
Author and physician

I loved Valentine's Day, because I knew that when we came to the dinner table it would be decked out in red, whether with a table-cloth, or with red plates, cups, and napkins. And there waiting for us at each of our places would be a small gift wrapped in shiny red paper, a small stuffed animal with a red heart, one of those little boxes of Whitman's candy, and a card.

I enjoyed these special meals so much that, after I was married, I started giving a couples' Valentine's dinner. Now it's a tradition for our close friends to gather at our house for an evening of lace and china, hearts and flowers, and little touches that remind us how much fun it is to be in love.
KAREN BALL
Author

My father worked with the railroad, and so was gone quite often. However, he usually bought us little gifts during his travels to use for special days, such as Valentine's Day. I will always remember coming to the dinner table on February 14 to find our chairs pushed in all the way, the seats covered by the tablecloth. When we would pull out our chairs to sit down, there would be a surprise gift—one most likely that Daddy had brought back from one of his trips—wrapped in red paper, placed on the seat of the chair, just waiting to be enjoyed.
PAULA SAPP
Pastor's wife

We always had the traditional Irish dish of mulligan stew on St. Patrick's Day. It's made with beef or lamb, has a thick broth, and includes potatoes, carrots, etc. Sometimes Mom would also make salt-risen bread. And once she put green food coloring in our milk—although that didn't go over very well!
ESTHER WALDROP

St. Patrick's Day

I had practically forgotten the existence of St. Patrick's Day until our older boys started school. Now on St. Patrick's Day we have green Jell-O and a devotional at our main meal of the day. Most often the devotional is on the life of St. Patrick, since his biography makes a good missionary emphasis. You could even follow his story with some stories of modern-day missionaries.
BRENDA POINSETT
Author

St. Patrick's Day wasn't a big holiday for a lot of people. In our house, however, it was the time we had meals where everything was green, from the Jell-O, to the broccoli, to the Green Goddess salad dressing, to the chocolate chip mint ice cream. And, of course, we all had to wear something green—although my dad was usually the most creative about this requirement. He would come to the table with a rose, leaves and all, or a blade of grass pinned to his shirt, or wearing some other unusual "green thing." Seeing his newest adornment always provided for even more laughter during a fun evening.

KAREN BALL
Author

Every St. Patrick's Day, my two children, now ages six and eleven, build leprechaun traps. They build little castles with trap doors (the castles are cardboard and oatmeal boxes; the flags are green construction paper) and tiny pots of pennies (cardboard circles) that they paint gold. Of course, they've never found a "little person" in the trap when they check it first thing in the morning on St. Patrick's Day. But they *have* found little green socks, tiny walking sticks, little reading glasses, tiny boots, little belt buckles, and other "little people" paraphernalia (thanks to our local toy store, which has a doll house department)—sure signs that one of the blessed little men *must* have been fooled long enough to make a stop.

COLLEEN MURRAY

April Fools' Day

Our family has a longstanding tradition of laughing together. My grandmother told me on my wedding day that as long as my husband and I could laugh together, we could weather any storm. Well, every single one of us in our family—my husband, our two sons, and myself—seems to be a natural born practical joker. So, as you can imagine, one of our favorite days of the year is April first. Every year, we have a contest to see who can catch whom first thing in the morning with an "April Fools' trick. I have had quite a lot of success catching our boys, especially when they were younger and I had the advantage of age and wisdom! However, when they reached their teen years, it became more and more difficult to catch them. Last year, I caught my fifteen-year-old son with one of the oldest tricks in the book. I short-sheeted his bed! It was such an obvious trick that he didn't even think to check, and we all had a good laugh. He even forgave me for playing my trick the night before April first.

This year, though, my son had his revenge. He came running into our room early on the morning of the first, shook me out of a sound sleep, yelling, "Mom! There's a policeman outside, and he wants to see you!" Groggily, I crawled out of bed, grabbed my bathrobe, and staggered to the door. When I pulled the door open, however, all that greeted me was a hand-lettered sign that read, "Gotcha!" My grinning sons and husband stood behind me and yelled "April Fool!"

These things may seem silly, but we have discovered that my grandmother was right. Laughing together does bring us closer.

LA VIDA HASKINS

Easter

You don't see this much anymore, but my dad always gets beautiful corsages for all "his girls." And he doesn't just buy all the same old standbys. Dad gets something that will match the outfit we are going to wear and if possible using our favorite flowers.

LISA MURPHY

One week before Easter we fill plastic Easter eggs with reminders of the last week of Jesus' life, including his crucifixion. A dime stands for the thirty pieces of silver. Thorns from our rosebush represent the crown of thorns. A nail is a must, of course, for the nail prints in his hands. Some whole cloves from my spice shelf represent the spices used to anoint Jesus' body. A small rock represents the stone that was rolled away. At mealtime each family member selects an egg, opens it, and tells the significance of the item tucked inside. There is something about touching the items and talking about them that makes the events of Jesus' last week real for all of us. By Sunday morning we are indeed ready to celebrate the Resurrection.

BRENDA POINSETT
Author

We celebrated Easter both with our core family and with our extended church family. The day started in the wee hours with a sunrise service, followed by our annual church Easter breakfast, at which the men donned aprons and fixed a veritable feast of eggs, pancakes (my dad was the master pancake turner), and ham. After breakfast, it was back up to the parsonage where my two brothers and I scoured the house for our Easter baskets (always a challenge, since my parents seemed to find more unexpected places to hide them every year). We attended church service, then the whole church family gathered at the home of Willard and Marie Clark. These two people were parents or grandparents to almost everyone in the church but us (though they willingly filled that role for us, too). There we children ran about, hunting Easter eggs to fill our colorful plastic buckets, knowing that somewhere on the property, possibly in the grape arbor or the tire swing, or nestled in the stone wall, was an abundance of candy eggs, plastic eggs filled with treasures, and one very special egg with each child's name on it. We ended the festivities by sharing a huge potluck dinner together.

KAREN BALL
Author

❖ Get up really early Easter morning and hang a banner across the front of your house that proclaims to the neighborhood, "HE IS RISEN!" If possible, make the banner yourselves—get the whole family involved. This will serve to remind your family and your neighborhood what this day is all about.

My mom would buy or make my three sisters and me matching Easter dresses and hats. Easter morning she'd leave them draped at the foot of our beds with pretty, new patent leather shoes to complete the outfit. It was like Christmas (only better because we were allowed to eat candy *before* breakfast!).   ESTHER WALDROP

When I was a child, we didn't have Easter baskets. Instead, we had Easter nests. Mine was always built in a brand-new pair of patent leather shoes, which were cleverly hidden someplace in the house by my mother. So when I found my nest, I not only got to enjoy my Easter surprises, I had a beautiful new pair of shoes to enjoy for the coming year.

PAULA SAPP
Pastor's wife

✤ Decorating eggs for Easter week is a fun, long-lived tradition. This year, use Christian symbols as you decorate eggs. Make eggs for each other with your names on them or special designs. Also, choose some of your special family friends and decorate eggs for them. Make up a pretty basket, and deliver it on their doorstep early Easter morning. Include a note of thanks from your family to your friends telling them how special they are in your lives.

We make a banner for Easter (and a similar one for Christmas) to remember and celebrate the true meaning of these holidays. The Easter banner has a hill and a path leading to the top of the hill. Starting with the first Sunday of Lent we add a brown circle (symbolizing the steps to the cross) to the bottom of the path for each Sunday though Palm Sunday. Then each day after that until the day before Easter another circle is added. On Easter morning we turn over the banner to reveal a picture of the risen Christ. You can make a banner like this out of felt, cloth, or simply construction paper. My son really enjoys adding things to the banner each day, and it gives us all an opportunity to discuss Christ's death and resurrection and what that means for all of us today.

DENISE ANDERSON

Springtime

Everyone in my family loves spring! From the moment the snow starts to melt, we all watch with anticipation for the first flowers to bloom and the leaves to start popping out on the trees. To celebrate this much-loved season, we set aside the first day of spring for a family walk together in the woods. We gather a bouquet of wildflowers, which we then take home and put in a vase in the middle of our dining room table. The color and fragrance serve to remind us that, no matter how dreary things may seem, there is always a new beginning just around the corner. URSULA REMINGTON

Every year we celebrate the first day of spring by doing a special activity together. One year we made kites and flew them in the park. Other years we have gone on picnics or gone out leaf collecting. It doesn't have to be anything big or complicated. It just gives us a chance to celebrate the approaching new season together.

SEAN FISHER

May Day

When I was a child, long before anyone associated May first with big military parades in Moscow's Red Square, May Day was a time of real festivity and fun. We children would plan our May baskets with care, collecting colored crepe paper, construction paper, small fruit containers, and other assorted containers that could be decorated with bright and cheery coverings. We tested our inventiveness for the containers, making cones from the construction paper, covering the small fruit containers with bright-colored crepe paper (which we would "flute" for added finesse), and creating handles from whatever materials were at hand (such as pipe cleaners).

Then we would fill these decorated "baskets" with flowers of the month—lilacs, lilies of the valley, tulips, etc.—and small candies.

The fun came in carrying these baskets to our friends' houses, hanging them on doorknobs or leaning them against the porch railings, ringing the bell or knocking, and running away to hide close enough to see the friends come out and find the baskets.

Simple pleasure, but one that made wonderful memories.

LUCILLE MARLAND LEONARD

My father courted my mother during the early spring. One of her fondest memories of their courtship is recorded in a faded picture where they are in a group of friends circling a maypole. While everyone else is holding his or her own streamer, my father gave his streamer away and came to hold Mother's along with her. It was his way of letting their friends know that he was serious about her!

So Mother always made a maypole for us when we were children. On the first day of May, she would tie streamers to a large birch tree in our yard, then gather the children in the neighborhood for the May Day dance. We would hold our colorful streamers high, going around and around while my mother sang and clapped her hands until the tree was wrapped in color. We got away from this tradition as we grew older, but when I fell in love, I talked my beau, David (now my husband), into coming to my house on May first. He and

I tied streamers to the birch tree, gathered my younger brothers and sisters and the neighborhood children together, and asked my mother to sing for us. She did so, holding Daddy's hand and smiling broadly, tears streaming down her face, as David and I danced with the children, holding one streamer in our joined hands.

ALICIA GREGSON

My mother grew up in a small farming town in central Illinois. They had a common tradition of giving May baskets to someone you care for on May 1.

I remember as a youngster helping my mother make the baskets out of woven strips of construction paper and decorated with cut-out paper flowers. They were then filled with popcorn, candy, and even sometimes little wrapped packets of homemade fudge. Then the basket was taken to the doorstep of my favorite boy that year. I rang the doorbell and ran the fastest I had run since last May 1!

Later, when I was out on my own, Mom would make the baskets every year for me and my roommates.

Now that I am married, every May 1 still brings baskets made with love and filled with wonderful goodies.   LOUANN WARD-BENSON

My mother loves it when each year we go to her house and plant her annuals such as petunias and marigolds for her.   RITA PAPALEO

Mother's Day

Mother's Day involved both my grandmothers and my mom. We'd all do something together that they enjoyed. Now my one remaining grandmother has difficulty walking so trying to find outings that both she and Mom will enjoy is a challenge. For the last couple of years we've found the perfect solution. They both enjoy fishing! We kids provide a picnic lunch, take them up to a small, private lake, bring gifts for each of them and spend the whole day there together. Grandma doesn't have to walk around, but it's still something Mom finds enjoyable.   LISA MURPHY

Mother's Day cards are always handmade at our house. Over the years they become quite a treasure trove of memories.

TIMOTHY R. BOTTS
Author and award-winning calligrapher

Breakfast in bed is recognized as a special occasion in our family. When our oldest daughter was three or four, we started to let her help make breakfast in bed for Mother's Day and Father's Day. She thought this was great and, after a few years, wanted to make breakfast herself. Soon she had a couple of helping hands in her younger sister, and she conveyed the significance of the event through the process.

This special act reached a high point this past year when our family was living with my wife's parents for a few months. In addition to making breakfast for their mother, Sarah, our oldest, made breakfast with her sister, Susan, and took it into the bedroom to her grandmother for Mother's Day. Grandma was very pleased to be included in this family tradition of ours without any prompting from the parents. It's a simple and enjoyable thing, as long as you don't mind the inevitable coffee stain or orange juice spill on your nightstand or bedspread—and it brings a lot of joy to the little ones.

MARK AND DEBBIE JEVERT
Missionaries, Youth for Christ/USA

Father's Day

We always tried to do something extra special for Mom and Dad on their special days. Sometimes we would make breakfast in bed for the honored parent. Other times we would try to surprise Mom by cleaning the whole house while she was out somewhere or wash the cars for Dad. We wanted to somehow show our thanks and appreciation for all *they* do every day without ever being asked and rarely being thanked.

CHRIS SPENCER

I used to dislike Father's Day because I didn't have one—it was just one more reminder that my father had abandoned my family and me. But now I can really enjoy it because I have a wonderful new dad. He usually gets to pick whatever he wants to do for the day with whatever he wants for dinner. When my grandfather was alive, the day would include him as well. My new dad grew up without a father also, so it makes our bond that much more special.   LISA MURPHY

When I was young, we always celebrated Father's Day with a special dinner. During the hard times of the Depression, our cards were homemade, but always told the profound respect and love we felt for our special dad. After his death, we discovered every card we had ever given him. They were carefully stored in his big desk drawer. His quiet appreciation of us was clearly stated in the legacy of that drawer!   GRACE H. KETTERMAN, M.D.
Author and physician

As a single mom of three sons for eighteen years I have many times claimed God's promise of being the "Father of the Fatherless." I've worked at instilling the concept of God being the "Perfect Father" by encouraging the boys to give a special offering to God on Father's Day.   JUDY SHANKS

David, our son, decided one year that he wanted to make a book for his dad, entitled "What I Love about My Dad." We got a small photo album, which he filled with pictures (some of the family, some taken from magazines), notes, and comments about what he loved about his dad. Needless to say, my husband was quite surprised—and touched—when he opened the gift. David enjoyed the project so much that he has done the same thing for the past several years. And we have enjoyed comparing the albums with each passing year, seeing the changes and growth in the relationship David and his dad share.   SONJA MARTINEZ

✤ **Carolyn Kilburn** and the families on her block celebrate a "Kid's Day" every year right after Mother's and Father's Days. Everyone chips in for food, drinks, decorations, and prizes. They devise simple games (e.g., beanbag toss, pin the tail on the donkey, horseshoes, egg toss, races, etc.), and have a big picnic

Kid's Day

together. The evening is ended by a dip in a neighbor's pool, and a gift time when each child receives a "Kid's Day" gift from his or her parents. Kids and adults alike have come to love this special day!

Independence Day

We love celebrating Independence Day in our house. We start out the day by decorating our mailbox and door with flags and streamers. We all dress up in red, white, and blue, and fix a veritable feast for a picnic lunch. After lunch, we attend any of the festivities the city is holding, and head for the city park to watch the fireworks display. We end the day by going back home and lighting sparklers, then holding hands and praying that God will bless and guide those who lead our country.
JULIE FORBES

❖ Fill your home with the sounds of freedom. Play Sousa marches throughout the day, or purchase a record or tape with a collection of patriotic songs. If you have a musical family, have a sing-along and belt out old favorites such as "God Bless America," "The Star Spangled Banner," "My Country, 'Tis of Thee," "This Land Is My Land," and more.

My earliest memory of the Fourth of July is listening to my father read the beginning of the Declaration of Independence. This memory never fails to stir me, so when I became a father I carried on this tradition. Now, our Fourth of July begins with those electrifying words:

"The unanimous Declaration of the thirteen united States of America. When in the Course of human events, it becomes necessary for one people to dissolve the political bands which have connected them with another, and to assume among the Powers of the earth, the separate and equal station to which the Laws of Nature and of Nature's God entitle them, a decent respect to the opinions of mankind requires that they should declare the causes which impel them to the separation.—We hold these truths to be self evident, that all men are created equal, that they are endowed by their

Creator with certain unalienable rights, that among these are Life, Liberty and the pursuit of Happiness." MORTON WINSLOW

Every Fourth of July, we would get up early in the morning and go outside to our flagpole. My father would offer a prayer for our family and the leadership of our country. Then my brother and I would unwrap the flag, hook it up, and raise it. At the end of the day, right at dusk, we would bring the flag down and fold it up again. This was a simple and sober part of our celebration, but it never failed to give me goose bumps. ADELE STEWART

❖ If you live near a beach, take your family there and build sand sculptures. Make a list of patriotic images (the Statue of Liberty, the flag, George Washington, the Liberty Bell, etc.), and make as many of them as you can. Then take pictures of the artists with their creations, and treat everyone to ice cream or some other refreshing goodies.

Thanksgiving

At Thanksgiving, our family gathers to read aloud *Thanksgiving at the Tappletons'*, written by my wife, Eileen Spinelli. At Christmas, we do the same thing, only we read aloud Barbara Robinson's *The Best Christmas Pageant Ever*. JERRY SPINELLI
Author, 1991 Newbery Medal winner for
Maniac Magee

Since all religions value this day, my family uses it as a time to include lonely strangers in a warm, family tradition by inviting them to come celebrate with us. Each year the menu is identical, bountiful and gracious. The blessings we have shared have come back to us from the countless friends we have met and maintained over the years. GRACE H. KETTERMAN, M.D.
Author and physician

Have family members write an ending to this sentence for every person at dinner: "I am thankful to God for you because . . . " These sentences are placed under each person's plate. Then, several times during the meal, everyone pulls out an affirmation note and reads it aloud. If you have children who are too young to write, have adults do the writing for them or help them draw a picture to show their thoughts.

Another idea is to pick ten people who have been especially important to your family that year. Send each person a homemade "You're special to our family" card.

MARLENE LEFEVER
Author

✤ In an article in *Charisma* magazine, **Jonathan Thigpen** shared this Thanksgiving tradition.

"Somewhere between the last bite of the cornbread dressing and the first bite of the pecan pie—that's when the basket is passed around each year at our family's Thanksgiving meal.

"We ask everyone present to drop in the basket, one at a time, the three small kernels of dried corn we've placed beside each dinner plate. With each kernel, we give one reason why we're thankful that day.

"Most often each speaker thanks God for someone else present while misty eyes around the table begin to glimmer in the candle-light. And when the guests go home in the evening, they inevitably comment: 'I want to do that again next year.'"

✤ Think of someone who will otherwise be alone on Thanksgiving Day. Perhaps you know of a college student who won't be going home for the holiday, or a widower with no family nearby. Invite him or her to your home to share your family's celebration of the holiday. Attend a worship service together, and later in the day ask your friend to stay and watch football or play games or whatever it is you would normally do. Make them feel like a part of the family for the day!

When the cool, crisp air announces fall's arrival, we anticipate Thanksgiving. Our annual reunion is held at our Lake Tawakoni house—within easy driving distance for everyone, including my brother, sister, and their families. The rustic, lakefront setting lends itself to outside fun. Since we do not have a television there, we spend time visiting and playing games. When the children were younger, they raked up piles of leaves and spent hours jumping in them. Now they can play volleyball, swing in the hammock, or paddle the canoe.

In addition to the warm family time, we love the aroma of hot spiced apple cider, turkey and all the trimmings, and often a fire in the wood-burning stove. Before our buffet meal, we stand in a circle, holding hands while Granddad prays. Then we sit around a cloth-covered Ping-Pong table that becomes our dining area. While we do see each other at other times during the year, everyone looks forward to our Thanksgiving reunion.

We were reminded of that last week while visiting our son at Texas A&M, and daughter at Baylor University. Each one wanted us to know they are planning to be home for our traditional day at the lake. My husband and I are grateful that our college students are interested in family fellowship.

FRAN SANDIN
Author

Editor's note: You know, Thanksgiving isn't the only time you can gather like this! Sometimes when a gathering is not in conjunction with a holiday, there is even more time to focus on family!

❖ Help your children appreciate the idea of Thanksgiving being a time of giving thanks—and what it means to be thankful for something. About a week before Thanksgiving Day, make a large paper tree out of brown construction paper. Then cut out several different colored leaves. Every day after dinner, give each person one leaf. Ask each one to write in a few words something they are thankful for and then tape it onto the tree. Help little ones by writing for them—or encourage them to draw a picture of what they are thankful for.

Christmas

On Christmas Eve, we enjoy a dinner of Chinese food each year. (Don't ask me how that tradition started, or more important, why?) Afterwards, grandparents, aunts, uncles, and cousins join us around the fireplace, and [my husband] Jim reads from the Bible. After discussing the passage, we do something very meaningful. The lights are lowered and I give each family member a votive candle. I explain as we take our turn igniting our candles that the light represents Jesus who was born into a dark world to give us eternal life. As each person lights his candle, he shares one blessing he is especially thankful for during the past year, and something he or she is asking God to do in his life the following year—perhaps a spiritual goal for the coming year. We then blow out our candles and Jim closes in prayer. The children then get to select and open one gift from under the tree.

SHIRLEY DOBSON
(from Let's Make a Memory, by Gloria Gaither
and Shirley Dobson, Word Books, 1983. Used by permission.)

With four married children, getting together as a family during the holidays soon became a challenge. Who would be where? After all, in-laws need visits, too. Our solution was to come up with alternate holidays. On odd numbered years, our family gets together on Thanksgiving, then the children visit the spouses' families for Christmas. On even numbered years, it's the reverse: the children go to the in-laws' for Thanksgiving, and the Hayford clan gathers for Christmas.

DR. JACK AND ANNA HAYFORD
Pastor and author; pastor's wife

❖ Here's a suggestion from *Good Housekeeping* magazine's etiquette expert, **Elizabeth L. Post**. On Christmas Day, the Post's four married children and nine grandchildren join them at their Vermont home. However, Mrs. Post and her husband found that things had gotten so hectic that they didn't have time to savor their presents to each other. Now the two of them give their gifts to each other on Christmas Eve, thus creating their own special time together and freeing themselves to give their full attention to their extended family on Christmas Day.

❖ Gather your family together around December 1 and discuss ways you can help make someone else's Christmas merrier. You could volunteer your services at a nursing home for a Christmas party, shovel snow for elderly neighbors, take someone Christmas shopping who doesn't have a car or can't get around well, gather food for a local pantry, work in a soup kitchen—the opportunities are endless. And most won't cost you much if anything at all; all that's needed is a willing heart and your time. Getting your children to start thinking about others at an early age and seeing you willingly—eagerly—giving of your time will lay the foundation for a generous, considerate adult.

In Sweden, custom dictates that the gift giver compose a poem and attach it to each item. The verse, usually quite humorous, half reveals, half conceals the contents of the package.

SWEDISH CHRISTMAS TRADITION

We open gifts Christmas Eve, but hold Christmas stockings until Christmas morning. I place the stockings on the foot of each person's bed while everyone is sleeping.

And we exchange *one* special gift on Christmas morning. In September, Dan and I and our two children draw each other's names. We then have a little more than three months to *make* a gift for the person whose name we've drawn. This fun idea stretches the mind but not the budget. Last year I drew Abigail's name, and I sewed a Raggedy Ann doll for her. Justin drew a picture, which we had made into a plate for Dan. Abigail, who was eighteen months at the time, made a handprint in plaster for me.

DAN AND DEBORAH COPELIN

When my children were younger, and excitement ran high prior to Christmas, we devised an entertaining game that kept them busily occupied for long periods of time.

Each year I kept pictures from cards received (they accumulate fast!). Subjects depicted on the cards were written on slips of paper: Santa, country scene, wise men, shepherds, the Christ Child, the words "Merry Christmas" or "Holiday Greetings," bell, animals, fireplace, wreath, candle, star . . . the list is endless. Participants then draw a slip of paper listing one of these categories. The cards were spread out on the floor, and the timer set for an agreed-upon period of time (two or three minutes worked fine). Then the scramble begins as each child tries to get the most pictures of his or her listed

subject. Sometimes scores were kept and the drawings continued until all categories had been chosen.   **SHIRLEY POPE WAITE**
Author

Editor's note: For added fun, you might have small wrapped gifts to be given as prizes for The Most Cards Gathered or Fastest Gatherer or Most Courteous Gatherer, or some other fun categories.

For now more than thirty years, my beautiful thirty-eight-year-old daughter (who has her own family) and I have had an annual "Saturday in December" Christmas "date." We set the day aside just for the two of us, go out for a lovely lunch together, do some Christmas shopping, drink some hot chocolate midafternoon, and thoroughly enjoy each other. It's a date neither of us would ever want to miss, and becomes a highlight of our holiday season.

TED W. ENGSTROM
President Emeritus, World Vision

Christmas was not so much a holiday at our house, as a season-long event. I always knew it was December when my two brothers, Kevin and Kirk, and I each would be given our own Advent calendar (a calendar with little doors that you open for each day of the year, revealing pictures or Scripture verses). Every morning, we opened the day's door, then showed each other the pictures or read the verses out loud.

Every evening, we gathered for Advent devotions. These centered around the lighting of the Advent wreath and special readings. My brothers and I took turns naming and lighting the candles (the Advent, Bethlehem, Shepherd, and Angel candles that went on the outside of the wreath, and the Christ Child candle in the center). When we were old enough, we took turns reading the devotions.

One tradition that I especially loved (and still do, when I'm home for Christmas!) was going Christmas shopping with my mom. She took each of us kids individually, so it was also a time of getting Mom all to yourself. We would head out, Christmas gift list in hand, for an evening of fun and laughter—and dinner out at the place of *our* choosing! Then, when we came home, we had to make a big production of getting the bags of gifts up to our room before Dad or the others could peek!

One year time was short. Kevin, my older brother, had left home for the Marines. So Dad took Kirk shopping, and Mom took me. I was thrilled because Mom and I were going to my favorite restaurant for dinner. Imagine our surprise when, after we'd been seated and had ordered, Dad and Kirk came into the same restaurant! Apparently it was Kirk's favorite place, too. We laughed and waved at each other as they were seated across the room. But the funniest moment came when, after watching us for a while, one of the waitresses came over, wished us a merry Christmas, and said she hoped Mom and Dad would "work everything out, because you seem like too nice of a family to be sitting on opposite sides of the restaurant."

On Christmas Eve, we always got to choose one gift to open— probably so we kids wouldn't explode from excitement. Then came the magic of Christmas morning. My favorite ritual was to creep downstairs in the wee hours of the morning to see the tree and the brightly wrapped treasures under and in it. When the clock finally reached an acceptable hour, we three kids would waken my folks (who had probably been asleep for all of two or three hours), and we'd all gather 'round the tree. First came our stockings. Then we'd pass presents out until everyone had a pile by their spots and we would go around the circle, opening our gifts one-by-one.

Like any kid, I enjoyed the fact that Christmas meant we got presents. But now, as I look back, I know that the best gift of all was one that I got every year—and it's a gift that I still cherish: an abundance of smiles and hugs, laughter and love.　**KAREN BALL**
Author

Creating a cupboard of special homemade sweets is a tradition of Christmas that extends into my earliest memories. The entire family helps make and decorate cookies, fudge, spiced nuts, and a host of other delicacies. When I was a child, my father sensed the impatience I felt at the endless wait for Christmas Day. With a wink and a crook of his finger, he would take me to the cold storage area and, ever so slowly, unwrap my favorite, giving me a precious piece of chocolate fudge. What a loving, fun tradition!

GRACE H. KETTERMAN, M.D.
Author and physician

Every Christmas we practice a variety of traditions. My wife, Harriet, the master baker, begins early in the season preparing about a dozen different Christmas cookies and candies. We always pick out a live tree. Everyone helps, including our boys—Schaun, twenty, and Michael, fourteen. But we wait for the coldest, wettest, iciest day in December. (This keeps the selection process moving.) On Christmas Eve, we enjoy a classy dinner with filet mignon, attend a candlelight church service, then come back home to exchange gifts—opening each gift one at a time, rather than a free-for-all. Opening gifts on Christmas Eve has also helped the Santa myth take care of itself. After the kids are in bed, the stockings are hung from most anywhere with care. This is our Christmas morning surprise. After pouring out the stockings, there's breakfast (waffles, perhaps) and afterwards we read the Christmas story from the Bible.

We also reminisce about the Christmas when Schaun, then three, insulted Santa at the department store. Santa was gleefully strolling along, passing out candy, when he walked up to us. From the shopping cart, in the nastiest voice I have ever heard Schaun use, came: "We want people to think of the baby Lord Jesus, *not you!*" Santa's cheeks got a little redder and he quickly moved on.

Our last tradition for the day is our afternoon calls to relatives on the West Coast.

JIM LONG
Editor, Campus Life magazine

In mid-December, the Rix family gathers on a weekend day for our annual Christmas Pancake and Cookie Bake. Grandpa Bill minds the stove top, flipper in hand, making English/Polish/Norwegian/Swedish pancakes, which are smothered in maple syrup or lingonberries. Grandma Jerri has been busy since about 8:00 A.M. making dough. As we arrive, she directs us to what still needs to be done. Brother Dave gets the whole event, brunch and cookie baking, on video.

After brunch, the dishes are cleared and the kitchen table is covered with tray after tray of cutout sugar cookies, just waiting to be decorated with red and/or green sparkling colored sugar, silver or multicolored candy balls, or chocolate sprinkles. Everyone gets into the act, either decorating or helping to make one of the numerous kinds of cookies (including almond crescents, cinnamon nut diamonds, and buttery spritz cookies).

The best part, of course, is the taste-testing when the cookies come out of the oven. We always hope for lots of broken or browned cookies, so we'll have a good excuse to eat them. When everything is done, we all bag the cookies up and everyone gets an assorted stash to take home for the rest of the holidays. JILL RIX

When we were children, we always started out Christmas Day by gathering at the table for Christmas breakfast. During the meal, we would open our stockings, which hung from the buffet in the dining room. Several times our eyes would drift to the doorway leading into the living room. Though the doorway was covered by a sheet, hung there by my mother so that we wouldn't see the tree and presents too soon, we knew there were wonderful surprises waiting for us. After breakfast, Mother removed the sheet, unveiling our beautifully decorated tree and the gifts that were waiting for us. We opened our gifts together, then Daddy would bring in the Christmas cards we had received that year, none of which had been opened yet. As we gathered around in a circle, he would open the cards, one by one, read each one aloud, then pass it around. Celebrating Christmas this way seemed to build our anticipation, and to make the enjoyment last all day long. PAULA SAPP
Pastor's wife

Both sides of our family have given us collectibles and keepsakes from our childhood, whether it be things we made when we were little, things purchased specifically for us, or special treasures endowed to us from Grandma or Grandpa. We wanted to give our girls the same kind of inheritance, so we started purchasing a special

Christmas ornament every year, specifically for them. As our girls have grown, they have taken great pride in "their" ornaments. They even have their own small trees in their rooms, which they decorate with their inherited ornaments, as well as with ornaments they make in school and church. When Sarah, our oldest daughter, leaves the nest, she will have a special collection of twenty to twenty-four Christmas ornaments that will make that first Christmas with her new spouse very special. And we hope this will be a legacy Sarah will pass on to her children, too.

Another Christmas tradition takes place on Christmas morning. We pause before we open presents, and Mark reads the Christmas story from Luke 2 to our three daughters. This simple act helps us remember the real meaning of Christmas as a family before we rip into the paper and the ribbon. Then we pray and thank God for the many blessings he has bestowed upon us as a family.

Our older two girls are now ten and six, and they have already caught onto this tradition. The year before last, Sarah, the ten-year-old, reminded her younger sister of our tradition, then brought Mark's Bible to the family room in anticipation of my reading. When these kind of small affirmations occur, you know that the heritage you are trying to instill in your children is starting to sink in. And that makes it worth the effort.   MARK AND DEBBIE JEVERT
Missionaries, Youth for Christ/USA

In our church, almost everyone except us was related! This created an atmosphere of family that has lasted to this day. Our church family loved Christmas, and every year we jumped wholeheartedly into our traditions.

One of the first events was our annual Christmas tree hunt. We all would gather at Willard and Marie Clark's home (the same place we went for Easter!), pile into a hay-filled wagon that was pulled by a bulldozer, and ride up an old logging trail into the mountains. (You just don't find better trees than they grow in the Oregon mountains!) Once there, we would fan out and choose our trees (in-between snowball fights), cut them down, tag them, and pile them in the wagon. The biggest and best tree was always the church Christmas tree. I can remember watching as my dad and other men from the church would climb to the top branches of beautiful, full pine or cedar trees and lop off the top seven feet for the church tree. Once the cutting and tagging was finished, it was back to the house, where we would find steaming cups of hot chocolate and still-warm homemade donuts waiting for us.

The week after our tree hunt, we all would come to the church for a decorating party. We would "deck the halls," and the tree, as we laughed and sang and joked together. Then would come our "Christmas Sharing Night," when each person brought something to share with the others. Over the years, the offerings have included stories or poems (some that the church members had written), songs (solos, duets, ensembles, whatever), songs played on instruments (baritones, violins, fiddles, harmonicas, flutes, pianos, etc.), and so on. After the sharing time, we congregated down in the basement to sample the Christmas goodies everyone had brought.

My favorite church tradition was our Christmas Eve candlelight carol sing. Before the service, my brothers and I would help set up and light candles throughout the church. To this day, the soft glow of candlelight stirs warm memories of sitting together and singing all our best-loved carols. At the close of the service, my dad would share a brief devotional, then we would end with a prayer. Now, every Christmas Eve, my husband and I try to find a Christmas Eve carol sing. But I have to admit that I've never found one that feels quite as wonderful as the Christmas Eve service at home.

KAREN BALL
Author

We have Christmas slumber parties, for both children *and* adults. We invite Christian friends from all over the country to come and celebrate the holidays with us. We also invite some families who are not Christian and try to give them a real happy image of what it means to be a believer. Our guests bring an array of wonderful dishes and tasty desserts, so we enjoy a true smorgasbord of delights. The time is filled with candlelight carol singing through-out the neighborhood, praying together, and just having fun. We have all kinds of games throughout the night with simple prizes (e.g., Tootsie Rolls, Post-It notes, etc.). One man told us how much it meant to him to be invited to a holiday event to which he could bring his children. In the morning, we relish a huge breakfast together.

We have enjoyed our slumber parties so much that we have even started having them on a smaller scale several times a year. These gatherings have been warm, special family and friend times.

THE FAMILY OF RON BALL
Author and entrepreneur

One of the traditions we celebrate at the Thigpen home is the giving of just three gifts to each other. We do this to honor the three gifts of the wise men to the Christ child—gold, frankincense, and myrrh. We match our gifts to the special meaning of each gift. The gold was a gift of honor and was very valuable. For us, our "gold" gift is one that is a very special "wish" type of gift. The frankincense was a fragrance that served a practical purpose. Thus our "frankincense" gift is one that makes your life more pleasant, but has a practical bent. The myrrh was a substance that had medicinal value for the people of the Middle East. It was a gift of something that was needed. For us, the "myrrh" gift is something that the person really needs, such as basic items of clothing. JONATHAN THIGPEN

Each year on Thanksgiving, Christmas Day, and Easter, we invite four or five single adults to join our family for dinner and the evening. One of these singles has been a retired missionary, now in her eighties; another, an Asian immigrant; others have been recently divorced persons or college students who weren't able to go home for the holidays. This is by no means a "charity project," either, for we and our children have been enriched by these special people!

RON KLUG
Author

When our children were young, each Christmas we decorated six trees: a large one for the living room and five small ones for each child's room. Each of the children would have to design and create his or her decorations and put them on his or her individual tree.

Then we all gathered in the living room to decorate the big tree together. I would make an inspection of all the trees and award prizes for the most beautiful, most original, most colorful, most heartwarming, most unusual—as you can guess, everyone got a prize. Then the following morning, on Christmas Day, we had the gift openings after breakfast.

Another tradition was that, at Christmas dinner, the youngest child got to sit at the head of the table next to Daddy. When it was time for the maid to bring in the next course, the child was told to press his magic nose and, at that precise moment, I would step on the buzzer beneath the table, summoning the maid, who immediately appeared. The older children, having already been through this, smiled knowingly at the pretense. ART LINKLETTER
Author, TV personality, and speaker

❖ **Jimmy and Rosalynn Carter** have enjoyed a tradition of trekking through their woods with their children to find a Christmas tree. Once they find "the tree," they bring it home and decorate it. They make the journey into the woods together, then all join in for the decorating. "Our tree may not always be the most beautiful one in town," Rosalynn comments, "but it's ours!"

We have made it a tradition to gather around a tape recorder each Christmas Eve and talk about the highlights of the past year. We have done this for nearly ten years now, and it is great fun to play tapes from Christmases past! CHRISTIAN OVERMAN
Author

Editor's note: If you have a video camcorder, you might try this idea with sight and sound!

At Christmas we find a family who has children that are not going to have a very happy holiday. Our boys each spend some of their money to buy gifts for these children. We add groceries and other gifts to this and we all go over and deliver the surprise to the family. The experience helps our children to realize Christmas is for giving.
D. CHARLES WILLIAMS, Ph.D.
Author

❖ Have a birthday celebration on Christmas Day? Of course, after all that's why we celebrate the day in the first place! Bake a birthday cake for Christ. Ask your children to help decorate it and even put candles on it. Then sing "Happy Birthday" to him!

Most of the women in my family are very busy with their careers, continuing education, involvement in organizations, and their own families. We rarely get together as a whole family during the year due to conflicting schedules. And we never really have time to bake on our own. So each year, we schedule two days to be together (as close to Christmas Day as possible). All the women—my grandmother, aunts, cousins—gather at Aunt Paula's house in Peoria. For two days straight—early morning until late at night—we bake thousands of cookies! We have many traditional recipes that we repeat each year; each woman is allowed to introduce a couple of new recipes to experiment on. There are tables all over the house of cooling cookies! When all the baking is done, we form an assembly line. Each woman takes a gift container and walks around filling it with one of each kind of cookie until the container is full. Then she picks up a new one and starts again from the beginning until all the cookies are packaged. These packages are distributed to friends, family members, and lots to Aunt Paula's church in Peoria. (Of course, we each get to take some home, too!) This is such a great time for us to catch up on the past year, really get our hands into a project, and collectively, cooperatively work together. HEATHER HILL

❖ **Leisa Thigpen** described this tradition in *Charisma* magazine:
  "We choose a tree ornament each year that symbolizes the most important family event of the year. Then we date each ornament. Over the years, the tree has become a family history book which we 'read' each Christmas season. Examples: a palm tree for a move to Florida; a tiny house for a new home; an alphabet block for a new baby."

❖ Gather a group of friends to go caroling. Not enough people continue this tradition anymore, but it is an excellent way to spread the message of Christ's birth to an audience already in the Christmas spirit.

We allow each of our children to purchase an ornament every year that is theirs to keep. While they live with us, it is displayed on our tree. But when they move out on their own, they'll be able to take their ornaments with them and have a good collection to fill their own trees. Hopefully these ornaments will bring back happy memories and make their new homes seem a bit cozier.   **PETER TAFT**

In Holland, on St. Nicholas Eve they follow the tradition of disguising some of their gifts in the head of a cabbage or in a gelatin pudding. Tiny surprises might be concealed in potatoes dressed as dolls. The more ingenious the disguise, the greater the fun!
                                                      DUTCH CHRISTMAS TRADITION

✤ Choose a present to take to a nursing home so someone else might be touched by the spirit of love and generosity. You may want to call first and ask the staff to give you the name of someone who has no family and would not get any gifts or visitors for the holidays. They may also be able to suggest an appropriate gift.

Our family's most meaningful tradition is that of Abend Essen or Christmas Eve supper. We started this as missionaries in Germany. We have a simple supper of German soup, sausages, bread and cookies. We eat by candlelight with background music of European cathedral bells and German carols. It helps us remember the simplicity of the first Heilige Abend [holy evening] when the Christ child came.   **EDA STERTZ**
                                                                 Author

When our youngest daughter was four months old we began recording each of the daughter's voices and our own at Christmas. That tradition started twenty-seven years ago and is still going. My husband usually starts by recording the outside temperature and where we are living (we moved a lot!). The girls would decide what they wanted to say before the recording. Sometimes they'd play the piano, quote a poem, read a Scripture verse, tell what they wanted or got for Christmas.

When our first daughter became engaged we began to include her fiancé on the recording. Two more sons-in-law have been added to the tape. The guys have invented some unique things to say. And eight years ago we began adding the grandchildren's voices.

Before we begin the new recording for the year, we play bits of all the years gone by. There are all kinds of groanings of embarrassment but they *love* to hear themselves! The grandchildren enjoy hearing what their mothers sounded like when they were small. We have worked on other traditions through the years, but this is the one that has stayed with us.

PAT BAKER
Author

Christmas is the time for worship. The carols we sing and the candles we light are expressions of our adoration to God for his precious gift. This year, how about using another art form for worship . . . as a *personal* worship expression? You may not consider yourself a poet, but here is a "formula" for writing a devotional poem that may draw from deep within your soul the feeling of Christmas in a new way.

First, think of every character in the drama of the birth of Christ, from the Annunciation to the flight of Joseph, Mary, and Jesus into Egypt. Pick someone who appeals to you in a special way. Then write what is called a cinquain, a five-line poem.

First line: Use a single word to name or designate a person involved in the birth of Christ.

Second Line: Use two words to describe or define the person chosen.

Third Line: Use three words to express action.

Fourth Line: Use four words that reflect your own personal feelings.

Fifth Line: Use one word that is a synonym for your person (see first line).

You may want to share your poem as a Christmas greeting, with your children, or your fellowship group, or you might use the idea as a group activity.

FELLOWSHIP OF ARTISTS FOR
CULTURAL EVANGELISM

Even though your family may not be together *physically* this Christmas, you can be together in spirit. **Kathy Haller** of Bloomfield, Connecticut, sends every family member an *oplatki* (Polish Christmas wafer), which they eat on Christmas Eve. Though miles separate them, they are sharing bread and the peace of Christmas.

❖ As you set up the nativity scene this year, take some extra time to make it a special event. Write down the name of your favorite Christmas carols, one for each figure in the nativity. If you can, match up the carol with the figure—for instance, "Away in a Manger" for the baby Jesus; "We Three Kings" for the wise men. Wrap each figure in tissue with the name of the carol. Then gather the family, and take turns choosing a wrapped figure from the box. As you place it in its special spot, sing a verse or two of the carol.

We have several young grandchildren, all of whom think they are destined for the stage! At Christmas they don their costumes—usually bathrobes, sheets, and towels, and reenact the events prior to the birth of Christ right up to the nativity scene. I am surprised how well they all memorize their lines right from the story in Luke!

JUNE OLSEN

❖ Don't rush around the house with Christmas ornaments and decorations this year, quickly placing them here, there, and everywhere as if you were racing to beat the clock! Take time to enjoy each piece for its unique beauty and history. If some items have special significance because they were passed down from parents or grandparents, be sure you tell your children the story so they will remember when someday those decorations are theirs! Even if it takes extra time to decorate the house this way, you'll find it much more enjoyable for everyone.

Start a tradition that shares your special Christmas memories from year to year. Take a plain wreath and attach to it items of special significance. A favorite snapshot, a vintage ornament, or a bit of ribbon can symbolize all the blessings of the holidays. You'll always "remember when" as you add souvenirs to your family's memory wreath. The baby's first Christmas, the year Santa brought a puppy, that first Christmas after moving to a new state, the time Aunt Margaret drove all the way from Florida despite an ice storm, Christmas dinner with a foreign exchange student—these are times that will never be forgotten. Create a sentimental wreath trimmed with stories to tell.

CHRISTY CRAFTON

Birthdays On the morning of our child's birthday, we light candles and wake up the birthday person by singing "Happy Birthday" by candlelight (even now that they're teenagers!). It's a great way to start the day and let the child know that "Today is a special day."

DAVE AND NETA JACKSON
Authors

Before each of our children were born, I bought each one a journal. I wrote each child a letter while they were still in the womb, telling them how and when we found out we were pregnant, how we felt, what we did to celebrate, etc. I wrote another letter on the day each child was born, telling them about the delivery, what they looked like, etc. For our daughter, we went into detail praising God for her miracle birth. I have written a letter to each child on their birthdays, filling the pages with funny things they have said and special moments for them throughout the year. It is my hope that, as they grow older, part of their birthday celebrations will include reading the journals. Ultimately I want the journals to become a heritage that they can pass on to their children, so that they can know how unique and special *their* parents were to us.

STEVEN AND LISA (WHELCHEL) CAUBLE

When somebody in our family has a birthday, everybody gets a present. These are called Unbirthday gifts and are generally inexpensive presents—as simple as a bright pair of shoelaces, a paperback book, or school supplies. As they say, it's the thought that counts. These gifts help keep everybody involved (especially young brothers and sisters) when the person who is the center of attention is surrounded by a mountain of gifts.

THE FAMILY OF RICK CHRISTIAN
Author and publishing agent

There is nothing I enjoy more than breakfast in bed on my birthday—except perhaps preparing breakfast in bed for my family members on their birthdays! Make something new or special. Bring in the meal on a tray with the newspaper, flowers, and be sure to sing a rousing round of "Happy Birthday." I'm not sure who enjoys it more, the person whose birthday it is or my children when they've helped prepare the meal!

JANET HAWKINS

Whenever a birthday came around, Mother would set little pewter candle holders with candles at each of our places. We would light the candles at the beginning of our dinner, and the one whose candle burned the longest (or sometimes went out the fastest) would get a little prize.

PAULA SAPP
Pastor's wife

❖ Birthdays for little ones don't have to be complicated or elaborate. How about making a simple and fun tradition of baking cupcakes for your child's birthday? Frost the cupcakes in the birthday child's favorite color, then decorate with sprinkles. If you want to add some variety, let the birthday child put on the sprinkles. Or set out a "buffet" of different toppings: M&M's, sweet tarts, gumdrops, jelly beans, tiny colored marshmallows, coconut, etc. and let your children have a decorating party.

We each get to choose what Mom makes for our birthday dinner. We also spend a lot of time decorating cakes to the specific interests of our children. For example, one year it was the head of Smokey the Bear because our son is an animal lover. Another year we did Raggedy Andy for our son—Andrew.

TIMOTHY R. BOTTS
Author and award-winning calligrapher

For the last few years, my friends and I have decided that we will give each other the gift of *self* for our birthdays. Rather than a store-bought gift, we give each other the gift of time together. For example, last year my best friend, Len, took me to the Aquarium/Oceanarium in Chicago. We took the afternoon off from work, then, on the drive to the city (an hour and a half, each way), we talked about our friendship and what we have seen the Lord do in our lives in the past ten years. Our time at the Aquarium was filled with fun, laughter, and amazement at the diversity of God's creative genius. As an avid fisherman, Len was able to share fascinating information and insights that went far beyond the (sometimes incorrect) identifying plaques above each tank. The drive home was another chance to talk and share.

I don't remember all the gifts Len has given me for my birthday in the years we've known each other. But I am sure I will always remember last year's gift because instead of just buying me a present, Len gave me something I can never get enough of: time with a treasured friend.

KAREN BALL
Author

❖ When your children are born, consider following the example of the Thigpen family. The father, Paul, makes up an original lullaby for the newborn during the first week of the baby's life. He always uses the child's name in the lullaby, then sings it to the child often.

When we kids were younger we would call all our parents' good friends from *all* over the country and invite them to a surprise birthday party for Mom and Dad (they have the same birthdate). We pooled our resources to buy streamers and balloons, and usually at least one friend from far away would be able to make the trip. My parents really seemed to enjoy it—sometimes they'd even act surprised!

ESTHER WALDROP

When I [turned] ten, instead of a pencil box, my father planted a tree, *my* tree. It was a Japanese maple—graceful as Baryshnikov, elegant as a Doric column—just the way, when one is ten, one hopes one will be too someday. I like to think it is still there, splashing the sky with scarlet. So plant a tree, waft a balloon into the air, make a memory—for isn't that what birthdays are all about?

EILEEN HERBERT JORDAN
Editor and writer

With seven children born in ten years, there weren't a lot of extras in our lives. Birthdays were scattered throughout the year with no two in one month, permitting us to enjoy Mother's special three-layer birthday cake with seven-minute boiled frosting throughout the year!

Our special treat was receiving the largest piece of our own birthday cake. In a large family we often shared one apple, one piece of dessert, amongst all of us. We soon learned to divide evenly and accurately.

But on our birthday we were always assured of having the largest piece of cake—no ifs, ands, or buts. Even after sixty-five years, the cherished memories make my mouth water.

ETHELYN THOMASON

Our family has a special birthday tablecloth that my mother made years ago. We use the special cloth only on someone's birthday. The person who is celebrating that day signs the cloth with the date and their age. Then my mother, and now I, embroider the name into the cloth using a different color for each person. What fond memories are invoked just by looking at the cloth. And when a family member gets married, a new tablecloth, thread and a hoop are our gift to them.

JANET HARRIMAN

❖ If you are reaching a milestone birthday, spending a birthday alone in unfamiliar surroundings, or if one of your family members is, here's an idea from writer **Kathryn Stechert Black,** who lives in Boulder, Colorado. Have your family and friends send you memories. Write them in advance and ask them to put in writing a special memory of a time you had spent together. (Be sure to ask them to put it in writing. If they call, you don't have something to look at over and over for years to come.) Friends may remember school days or summertime fun. Family can go back to the day you were born, your baptism, things you don't remember at all. Some people may even send little mementos or photos. And all of this together makes a treasure to savor and a tangible reminder that you are connected.

On our birthday, we could always count on having an angel food cake *and* a sponge cake. This was because Mother used the whites of the eggs to make the angel food cake, and the yolk to make the sponge cake! Also, when Mother made our birthday cakes, she baked little treasures into the cake, each of which had a special significance. For example, she always baked a little ring in the cake. The person who got the piece of cake with the ring in it, according to tradition, would be the next one in the family to fall in love and get married! This always added to the spirit of fun during our birthdays. And it brought quite a few laughs, depending on who was the lucky person to find the ring!

PAULA SAPP
Pastor's wife

A child whose birthday falls during the Christmas season can feel slighted or upstaged. Our daughter's birthday is on December 19, and we developed a tradition that combines her birthday with Christmas. On the nineteenth, we set up the Christmas tree, and the whole family decorates it. Then we have a family supper by the tree and give our daughter her birthday gifts.

RON KLUG
Author

In our family, birthdays were a day of real celebration, from beginning to end. In addition to being given a party attended by friends and family, the birthday person got to choose a family activity for the day (our choices have included going to the beach or the mountains, going to a movie, flying kites, or going on a picnic). The birthday person also chose what we would have for a birthday meal—whether something home-cooked (my favorite was Mom's Bar-B-Q chicken on the grill!) or something at a favorite restaurant. So for us, the anticipation, celebration, and sense of being really special lasted all day long.

KAREN BALL
Author

When a child is born into our family, my parents—the child's grandparents—create a "time capsule." Included in this package are items that give a picture of life at that time. Here arc some of the kinds of things you'll want to think about including: a local newspaper, a national newspaper, *People Weekly* magazine, a fashion or sports magazine, a baseball cap from the World Series winners that year, best-selling album or single, political campaign buttons. Any memorabilia that would be fun to reminisce over in twenty years. Then plan to have a special birthday party for the child when he or she turns twenty-one. Open the capsule and enjoy the "artifacts" together . . . then pack them away for another special occasion.

MARK MACDONALD

Anniversaries

For our anniversary we go to a nice restaurant with a quiet corner. As we eat, we celebrate the number of years we've been married in this way. We choose one theme for the night, then, starting with the first year, we go through the years (twenty-three of them now), taking turns to share. Some of our themes have included the year's:

1. Greatest event
2. Funniest event
3. Most spiritually uplifting event
4. Most challenging event
5. Hardest event and its victory
6. Event that changed me most

Now that we have so many years to talk about, we alternate, with Charles taking one year, and me taking the next. But in the early years, we both shared our memories about each year. This takes us through both tears and laughter and helps us see all the good . . . and all the God!

CHARLES AND BARI HILL
Directors, Family Life Mission,
Springfield, Missouri

We repeat our wedding vows to each other on our anniversary. It is a tangible way of remembering the special day of our wedding, and of reaffirming those sacred words we pledged to one another. We also have a cassette tape of the wedding and we occasionally listen to it and talk about our memories of the ceremony.

As our children grow older and look through the photo albums of our wedding, they ask questions and make comments on them. They also have seen our vows (we have them framed in our home), and have asked questions about what they mean and why we said them. Their interest particularly peaks after we have been to a wedding together as a family, and they see it in real life.

In a day where commitment and "till death do us part" seem to mean less and less, our girls seem to find comfort knowing that their mom and dad have told them they will never get divorced. The reality is that the promises we made to one another when we were married are just as real today as they were back then.

MARK AND DEBBIE JEVERT
Missionaries, Youth for Christ/USA

From the first year they were married, my father sent my mother a special anniversary gift: one rose for each year they had been married. When I was old enough to count, it became my "duty" to count the roses, making sure the florist had gotten it right—though I'm sure Mother wouldn't really have cared if the florist had missed one or two. What mattered most to her was that Daddy never once forgot.

PAULA SAPP
Pastor's wife

❖ For your anniversary this year, try playing the "Do you remember?" game. Each one of you make a list of events from your courtship, wedding, and years of marriage. Then say, "Do you remember the first time I saw you?" and have a contest to see who can remember the most details.

Weddings We plant trees at weddings on our farm and also on other special occasions. My daughter and son-in-law planted four fruit trees at their wedding and now my grandchildren are climbing the trees and picking the fruit!

DR. JOYCE BROTHERS
Author and psychologist

❖ Just before their marriage in 1992, **Connie Sellecca and John Tesh** were interviewed. During that discussion they disclosed that they had chosen premarital abstinence during their year-long romance—for religious reasons and "to be a good role model" to Sellecca's son, Gib, who was ten at the time. She said, "Our honeymoon will be traditional in every sense of the word."

When Tesh and Sellecca were married, the couple exchanged the traditional gold wedding bands. In addition, they gave Sellecca's son a ring. It was inscribed with the words "We are a family."

This is a good way to include a spouse's children from a previous marriage and make them feel like they too are a part of the union that is taking place.

One afternoon, my sisters and some cousins were sitting around talking about our weddings. We all agreed that it was frustrating to have spent the time and money we did on a dress that we would only wear once in our lives. That's when Mary, my sister, came up with the idea of "Wedding Dress Reunion." We all agreed to a day and place (our house), then pulled out our wedding dresses, our pictures, and any other mementos that we had from our weddings. My aunt makes cakes for people, so she baked and decorated a wedding cake. My youngest cousin, who has only been married a year, brought her bride and groom decoration to top off the cake. My daughters and I decorated our entryway with wedding decorations and white balloons, and my son acted as the official photographer. Everyone came early on the day of the reunion, so that we could get dressed together. That first reunion was so much fun that we agreed to do it again the next year. To date we've had five "Wedding Dress Reunions," and we're looking forward to our sixth!

ALICE MONTGOMERY

QUOTATIONS FOR REFLECTION

Lift your glad voices in triumph on high,
For Jesus hath risen, and man cannot die.   HENRY WARE, JR.

God could not be everywhere, and therefore he made mothers.

OLD JEWISH SAYING

All I am, or can be, I owe to my angel mother.

ABRAHAM LINCOLN
Sixteenth U.S. president

When I was a boy of fourteen, my father was so ignorant I could hardly stand to have the old man around. But when I got to be twenty-one, I was astonished at how much the old man had learned.

MARK TWAIN
Author

A child's glory is his father.

PROVERBS 17:6, TLB

The God who gave us life, gave us liberty at the same time.

THOMAS JEFFERSON
Third U.S. president

Thou has given so much to me. . . . Give one thing more—a grateful heart.

GEORGE HERBERT
Poet

Love begins at home. If we do not love one another who we see twenty-four hours [a day] how can we love those we see only once?

MOTHER TERESA

Thanksgiving Day . . . the one day that is purely American.

O. HENRY
Author

Time is a threefold present: the present as we experience it, the past as a present memory, and the future as a present expectation.

ST. AUGUSTINE OF HIPPO
Church father and philosopher

Only love lives forever. **POPE JOHN PAUL II**

Keep company with the more cheerful sort of the Godly; there is no mirth like the mirth of believers. **RICHARD BAXTER**

The fact of Jesus' coming is the final and unanswerable proof that God cares. **WILLIAM BARCLAY**
Author

Father Francis Mulcahy: "The first rule of orphanages and Irish families is there's always room for one more."
FROM TV'S "M*A*S*H"

It is good to be children sometimes, and never better than at Christmas, when its mighty Founder was a child Himself.
CHARLES DICKENS
Author

Christmas is the season for kindling the fire of hospitality in the hall, the genial flame of charity in the heart. **WASHINGTON IRVING**
Author

One of the great similarities between Christianity and marriage is that, for the Christians, they both get better as we get older.
JEAN REES

Our Lord has written the promise of the Resurrection, not in books alone, but in every leaf in springtime. **MARTIN LUTHER**

A happy marriage is the union of two good forgivers.
ROBERT QUILLEN

Of his marriage ceremony to fellow born-again Christian, actress Connie Sellecca:

I started to cry when I saw Connie, 'cause she was so beautiful. So I bit the side of my mouth to stop. I kept thinking I got real lucky, and God was the one that did this.

JOHN TESH
Musician, composer, cohost
of TV's "Entertainment Tonight"

Easter, like all deep things, begins in mystery and ends, like all high things, in great courage.

BLISS PERRY

CHAPTER THREE

Traditions for Day to Day

This is the day the Lord has made; let us rejoice
and be glad in it.

PSALM 118:24

Would to God that we behaved ourselves well in this world,
even for one day.

THOMAS À KEMPIS

*M*y husband, Don, is a real stickler for regular maintenance with our cars. Sometimes I find this frustrating—until I realize that we have a ten-year-old car that still looks and drives almost as well as it did when it was new. Without my husband's sometimes daily care, that car would have gone the way of the wreck heap long ago. Instead, we have a vehicle that works fairly well despite its age. ❖ A family needs daily maintenance, too. There are lots of day-to-day nuts and bolts kinds of things that need to be considered and handled. Funny thing is, you don't notice how important these things are until they don't get done. Then, suddenly, everything seems to be in a mess! The following traditions don't have anything to do with holidays, special events, or anything specific. They simply grew out of the "maintenance work" of building a family. But they offer some creative ways to smooth out any rough spots in the way your family operates— and to keep your family from finding itself on the "wreck heap." ~KMB

Mealtimes   Family dinners were a tradition in my home. Though we were a large family, Papa and Mama insisted that we have *at least* one meal together each day—usually this was dinner. It was here, around the table laden with exquisite cooked delicacies, that we shared the day's adventures . . . the tears, the laughter, the trials and the glories. It was here that we learned of our family history and the inspiring story of my parents' immigration to America. The closeness that these dinners engendered has lasted a lifetime and was responsible for giving me the sense of what being a "family" truly means.

DR. LEO F. BUSCAGLIA
Author

Our family goes out to dinner quite often. For the past twenty years our four children, their friends, and my wife guess the amount of the check. The closest to the actual amount gets $1.00—the amount has never changed in twenty years! Our children are now 28, 26, 24, and 21, but they still insist on guessing the amount of the check. I love to eat out with my family because we just sit and talk for a couple of hours with no interruptions. We then end with someone who has a problem he or she would like to bring up for discussion. If one person has a problem it is up to the entire family to try to come up with suggested solutions. This is a very tangible way of showing each other how much we care.

LOU HOLTZ
Head football coach,
University of Notre Dame

When asked if her children—ages seventeen, fifteen, and twelve—really *talk* with their parents, **Marilyn Quayle** responded: "Oh, yes! And I think it's because we've always eaten dinner together. From the time they were in high chairs, they've always been at the dinner table. If I could pinpoint one thing that could help families, it's taking time to sit down together at dinner. Start when they're little—when they don't have a lot to say, but you have a lot to offer them—and show them you care about their day and make conversation. Teach them table manners. Our kids are disappointed if we don't eat dinner together."

❖ Use supper as your family meal. Agree together that everyone will eat supper together. Go around the table and find out how each person's day has been. Consider choosing one day a week for Activity Night after supper. Once the meal is over and the table has been cleared, do something together around the table. For example, play a game, put a jigsaw puzzle together, write letters to a grandparent, make cookies or a pie, etc.

We have a tradition of long standing (and obscure origin) of reading the dictionary after Sunday noon dinner in the dining room. (Of course, our Sunday dinner is a tradition in itself, with the table all decked out with the good china and silver.) One Sunday when our children heard my husband and me exclaiming over the obscure meanings of words on our lists, gleaned from reading during the week, they began bringing their own words to look up. When my husband recently had to be gone for an extended period of time, our seventeen-year-old son took his place by reading the dictionary on Sundays.   **DONNA FLETCHER CROW**
Author

Who gets to sit in the dining room chair with the arms? At our home, the person who's had the best or worst day gets that special honor. Deciding who sits in the "special chair" promotes communication about each person's day.

**THE FAMILY OF JAMES AND
LOIS WATKINS**
Authors and pastors

At our dinner table we keep an old recipe box with 3x5 cards, as our Prayer Box. On the cards, we write down people's names and requests that we want to pray for (one request per card). After we finish eating supper, each person in the family picks out one card from the front of the file and prays for that request. Then the card

goes in the back of the file. Our teenagers often add the names of their friends to the file. The Prayer Box is a meaningful way for our whole family to bring our concerns for relatives, friends, neighbors, and various issues to God in prayer.   DAVE AND NETA JACKSON
Authors

Teatime probably is the tradition for which our family is best known. Friends of all ages angle for invitations, and our children's friends "just happen" to show up around 3:30 in the afternoon. It all happened when we were blessed with a daughter after our three lovely sons all were in school. As soon as Elizabeth could hold a teacup, I began having tea parties with her. It didn't take her nine-year-old brother long to catch on to the fact that we weren't just having tea—there were goodies, too.

John soon began bringing his friends home after school. When I became disturbed over less than perfect manners, I spoke to my children quietly. I will never forget the delight of hearing my son lecture a table of ten-year-olds: "Look, guys, tea time isn't for grabbing food. It's for relaxing and sharing about your day. And you don't start eating until the hostess has finished pouring!" Those little boys are now eighteen, and you should see their manners!

DONNA FLETCHER CROW
Author

One tradition is our Saturday morning breakfast. After a week of self-serve, eat-on-the-run breakfasts, Saturday morning is always a family sit-down meal of blueberry pancakes and sausage.

THE FAMILY OF JAMES AND
LOIS WATKINS
Authors and pastors

On Sundays, we try to leave a big meal cooking in the oven or in the Crock-Pot while we go to worship. This way, we can invite visitors home for lunch. The look of surprise and delight when first-time visitors to our church get invited home for a meal (especially college students or single people) is worth the extra work—and it's often the open door that brings visitors back again.

But one weekend, half of our family was away, so I was thinking in terms of hot dogs after church for my daughter and me. Wouldn't you know it, we sat down next to two college students visiting our church for the first time! So—I invited them home anyway, and we had great fellowship over hot dogs and leftovers!

DAVE AND NETA JACKSON
Authors

We can't seem to get through a dinner without looking something up in a reference book. We're talking away, and suddenly we just have to know what the capital of some country is, or who wrote a famous line, or which way the dessert fork is supposed to point. Now we have a bookcase for the dining room to hold a dictionary, anthologies, an etiquette book, history books, an atlas, a Bible, art collections, and all the other books we can't get through a meal without.

LAVONNE AND DAVID NEFF
Editors

We have three small girls, with the oldest now ten. They like to know what to expect and that they can depend on certain things in life. It is a family tradition to have Dad cook popcorn for the family on Thursday night (which means they get to stay up an extra half hour), to have Mom make pancakes on Saturday morning, and (if finances allow) to have pizza on Sunday night.

These three "regular" meals are a highlight for our girls, and help remind them of the importance of completing tasks (remember, if you don't get ready for bed by 7:30, no popcorn tonight!). Of course, hectic schedules often throw a curve into these traditions, so we try to be flexible and shift these special events when change is inevitable.

MARK AND DEBBIE JEVERT
Missionaries, Youth for Christ/USA

Walter and I wanted to teach our children to have a thankful instead of a complaining spirit. We prepared a little box with a slit in it and called it our "Thanksgiving Box." We instructed our children that any time during the week, when something good happened to them, they should write on a little slip of paper what it was and why they were thankful. This idea caught on quickly from our youngest who was not quite six to our oldest who was beginning junior high. I can still remember the happy moments at our Saturday evening meal when the oldest child was asked ceremoniously to open the "Thanksgiving Box," and to read the slips of paper inside. Our children loved to invite their friends to be present during this little celebration. Over the years this tradition brought us—and our guests—a great deal of joy and helped us to focus not on the things that made us unhappy, but on the things that caused us to rejoice.

INGRID TROBISCH
Author and speaker

❖ No matter how busy your schedules are, take time for your kids and for each other. Few people's schedules are as busy as that of an NFL coach. For **Tom Landry,** former coach of the Dallas Cowboys, that meant a lot of time away from home. However, Landry made a point of being there when he could for his children and wife. "Even during football season," Mrs. Landry says, "when coaching was a seven-day-a-week job, he ate breakfast with the kids every morning, and he'd always be home for dinner with the family. And one night a week, he and I would go out."

Once a month we go out to a restaurant for dinner. That gives my wife a break from the kitchen, and the rest of us a break from having to clean up!

BRYANT PHILLIPS

Bedtime At bedtime, one of our friends tucks his kids into bed with a private whisper: "I'm so glad you're you!" "I love your hugs," or "Jesus loves you, and so do I!" How do we know this? Our daughter spent the night at their house, and received her own "whisper" from the daddy of the house.

DAVE AND NETA JACKSON
Authors

Bedtime prayers were special times when we were little. My parents taped it once; listening to it now as an adult is really something! Such purity and innocence when you're five years old. The weight of the world is not yet on your shoulders. Your biggest concern is, "God, please bless the kitty, too."   LISA MURPHY

Sick Days

Being sick is never fun for anyone. However, as parents we can take some of the sting out of it by being there, loving, caring, and giving our children something to look forward to in the midst of rough times. In our family, sick children can count on homemade chicken soup and many-flavored Popsicles. Somehow this tradition acts as a distraction during long days, and it serves as a reminder of tender loving care received from Mom and Dad.

JOSH AND DOTTIE MCDOWELL
Authors and speakers

Bible Reading

One of my earliest memories is that of seeing my grandmother and grandfather reading their Bibles together. They would sit at the table after dinner and read together. Often either my mother or father would join them, while the other sat with us children, telling us Bible stories. We children knew that my grandparents' Bible reading was a special time for them and that we were not to disturb them. When I was old enough to join them, I was given my own special chair at the table and my own Bible, a children's Bible, to read. I also had paper and crayons at my place, where I could draw pictures from the story I had just read.

This simple method helped me to realize early on that the Bible was a vital and necessary part of everyday life.   JAMES RENN

One day while visiting my grandmother, I remarked that with two toddlers I couldn't seem to find time to read the Bible. She said she had fought the same struggle when she had small children, and had come across a rather unique solution. She bought a smaller sized Bible, and kept it in the master bathroom of their house, on the back of the john! Then, whenever she was in the bathroom, whether for a bath or for brushing her teeth, she would read a small portion of Scripture before she left the room.

I laughed, but I gave it a try—and it works! Now when I do my "getting ready for bed" ritual every night, I have one added step: I read a chapter from the Bible before I turn the light off and head for bed. It is the first method that has really worked for "finding time" to read the Bible regularly—and it is a great way to get my thoughts onto the Lord before I sleep.   BARBARA BEEKMAN

Without a doubt, the most exciting and important tradition with our family is memorizing Scripture together. If we could give one gift to every family in the country, we would give them the gift of memorizing Scripture together. Here's the formula for doing this (and it works better than Gerber's on a baby and is more effective than Ralph Lauren with a teen):

First, get into the Word daily. Mom and Dad have to get excited about God's Word. When your kids see you having quiet times with the Bible, they get the idea you live with your nose in God's Word. Second, memorize *chapters* of Scripture rather than just verses. Take it a verse at a time, of course, but don't move on when one or two verses are set. Memorizing only individual verses can keep you from the deeper meaning, emotion, and drama that come from understanding the context. Third, feed the Word to your kids, starting tonight, by memorizing a passage together. Age three is a good time to begin; age ninety isn't too late to start! Fourth, apply God's Word to your life, and help your kids to apply it to their lives throughout the day. Fifth, center your family devotions around the Scripture that you're learning. Have the kids take turns leading in this devotional time.

The more you memorize and meditate on Scripture, the more meaningful it is. And the more meaningful it is, the easier it is to memorize and think about it. It's a wonderful cycle.

JOE AND DEBBIE-JO WHITE
Author, speaker; owners/directors of
Kanakuk-Kanakomo Kamps

❖ Have each member of your family choose a favorite verse. Then make banners out of those verses to put on the door or wall of your rooms. Have a contest, too, seeing who can memorize their verse first. The best and surest way to learn the love of Jesus is through the family.

✤ It's never too early—or too late—to make reading the Bible a part of your daily routine. When the Johnson family comes to the dinner table, Mr. Johnson reads for ten minutes before the meal is served. The Fosters gather in the living room after the evening meal for fifteen minutes of family Bible reading. The Wilsons take fifteen minutes just before bedtime, when the children are already scrubbed and in their pajamas, for Bible story time. Ron and Judy Welkane work for the same company. During their morning drive to work, Ron drives and Judy reads the Bible out loud.

You, too, can start to use an already daily activity to help you read the Bible regularly.

When our kids were young, I would gather them at bedtime for a Bible story. It increased their interest when I'd let them choose the story from a Bible storybook. After the story, first I would pray, and then they would pray. As our children entered junior high, though, I wanted *them* to develop the practice of Bible reading and prayer. So I bought each child a suitable version of the Bible and encouraged them to continue on their own what we'd done for years together.   BONNIE RICE

Devotions

At night we all gather in the boys' room and pray together. It's also our time to just talk about what's gone on that day and be together as a family with no interruptions. When I was growing up we were able to have devotions after supper every night without fail. These days schedules are too hectic—my husband is a doctor—so we count on that time before bed to be our family time.
                                                          CYNTHIA ANDERSON

When we are planning a long trip we choose a book of the Bible that has the same number of chapters as days in our trip. Every day at lunch we read one chapter and talk about it. It is a break from normal daily devotions—just as a vacation is a break from normal daily routines!   PHILIP ASPEGREN

We found it hard to hold family devotions every day. So now we concentrate on having one meaningful "Jesus Time" each week.

Our children, ages five and seven, like it best when they get to act out Bible stories. So first we read the story of, say, David and Goliath. Then they pretend to be David selecting five smooth stones and boldly marching out to protect God's honor. One bonus is that my wife and I get involved, too. Not to mention that I make a great Goliath!

KEVIN MILLER
Editor, Christian History magazine

We have a half dozen graces we sing throughout a month alternating these at mealtime with conventional prayers. (The rewards increase as our boys get older and their voices change!) This keeps mealtime prayers from becoming routine. We also pray for the people from whom we have received mail that day and read missionary letters together. As the kids became teenagers we found it increasingly difficult to have devotions from books, so we've been using page-a-day calendars. When there is time we discuss the verse and pray, responding to God about the meaning of the verse.

TIMOTHY R. BOTTS
Author and award-winning calligrapher

Prayer ❖ Take a few minutes each night before you and your spouse go to bed to stop in each child's bedroom and pray together for that child, asking God to guide, watch over, and bless that child. Before leaving the room, thank God for the unique gift he has given you both in each child, and ask him to help you see each child through God's eyes.

I'm not sure when the custom started or how it came to be, but it is one of our family traditions that has endured. Behind my chair in the dining room is a shelf on which we keep a daily devotional book. For the last five years or so, the devotional book has served as sort of a paperweight for the hundred or more Christmas cards we receive every year. My wife and I both work, so our hectic schedules don't permit a prayer time together in the mornings. Instead, each evening after the dinner dishes are cleared, we read a portion from the Scriptures from our devotional book, and then take one of the Christmas cards from the top of the stack and make it a part of our prayer time. Sometimes the cards provoke more than prayers. Many times after our prayer time . . . I pick up the phone and call the friend. Often the calls have proven providential. Sometimes instead of calling, I go back to my desk and write a short note. Many times a note has come back, renewing love and always warming our hearts. "You prayed for *me?*" I tell them about our Christmas card custom and often our friends report that our prayers came at a time when they were truly in need.

WIGHTMAN WEESE
Author

We have always asked grace over our meal when we eat in restaurants. Invariably asking God's blessing on our food—and on every hand that prepared it—makes for a valuable witness in the market place.

IRENE BURK HARRELL
Author and publisher

From an interview conducted by Dale Hanson Bourke for Today's Christian Woman *magazine:*

"I can pray over my kids. That's about all I can do. Not that prayer is an insignificant thing at all. I pray that God gives me the right attitudes in raising them while they're at school. This journey of motherhood is never ending. I talked to my mom the other day, and she said that even when your kids are grown, you still keep praying. Motherhood may take on different forms, but it never ends."

SANDI PATTI
Singer

FAMILY PRAYER

Lord, behold our family here assembled.
We thank you for this place in which we dwell,
for the love that unites us,
for the peace accorded us this day,
for the hope with which we expect the morrow;
for the health, the work, the food and the bright skies
that make our lives delightful;
for our friends in all parts of the earth.

Give us courage and gaiety and the quiet mind.
Spare us to our friends; soften us to our enemies.
Bless us, if it may be, in all our innocent endeavours;
if it may not, give us the strength
to endure that which is to come
that we may be brave in peril,
constant in tribulation, temperate in wrath
and in all changes of fortune
and down to the gates of death,
loyal and loving to one another.
As the clay to the potter
as the windmill to the wind
as children of their sire,
we beseech of you this help and mercy
for Christ's sake.   ROBERT LOUIS STEVENSON

✣ Post a map of the world on the wall of your kitchen. Mark with a star the countries/cities where you know a missionary. These can be missionaries supported by your church or denomination, friends or family members, anyone you know who is serving God's kingdom in this capacity. Then number each star and make a chart of who is in what city/country; post the chart next to the map. Each day at breakfast or dinner—whenever the whole family is together—have someone choose a number and that is the missionary you will pray for in a special way at that meal. Be sure to have that same person point out on the map where that country is. Not only are you promoting prayer support of missionary work, but you may all learn some valuable lessons in geography!

I've become very aware of the power of prayer. My grandmother still prays for me, and I have no job that's more important than praying for my family.

   If every woman would take ten minutes each day to pray for her family and her country, I know we would see change.

                                        DENIECE WILLIAMS
                                        Singer

By the time children are five, their parents will have done at least half of all that can ever be done to determine the children's future faith.

RANDOLPH MILLER

Thinking that three hours of any movie are harmless for the child but two hours of church and Sunday School are too much for his nervous system is just bad thinking. Giving him a nickel for the collection and a dollar for the movies not only shows a parent's sense of value but is also likely to produce a proportionate giver.

ZION'S HERALD MAGAZINE

Saying, "I Love You"

My wife, Lillian, and I started a new tradition called "Son-in-Law Appreciation Dinner" ten years ago when Sue, our daughter, was married. Each spring, not always on the same day, we have a special meal for Doug, Sue and their children. Sometimes it is at our home and sometimes we go to a restaurant. During the meal we tell him we love him and what we appreciate about him. I might say, "Doug, I appreciate the way you are so gentle with Sue and the children. You're a good dad. Your kids love to play ball with you." Then we end the evening by giving him gifts.

PAUL WELTER, ED.D.
Author and counseling psychologist

Editor's note: Wouldn't it be particularly meaningful if the gifts were personally made by the giver?

I live with my parents, and at least once a week my dad brings both my mother and me fresh flowers. He usually leaves them in our bedrooms with a card or note. There is no special reason for doing this—just that he loves us!

LISA MURPHY

❖ Choose one day a week as Building-Up Day. Throughout the day, leave notes of encouragement for family members in different places around the house. Some key spots: on the mirrors in bathrooms and bedrooms, on the TV, in a book someone is reading, on a pillow, in a lunch pail, taped to a hanger in a closet, pinned to a coat, in the medicine chest, in a shoe, taped to the steering wheel of a car, and so forth.

A daily occurrence at our house is what we call our "famous three-way hugging spree." When my husband, who is a district-court judge, is ready to leave for court in the morning, he and I and our daughter embrace in a tight circle to ask God's guidance, wisdom, and protection for our day. The last words my husband hears as he heads out the door are "Love you, Daddy!"

One morning, 'Guerite (pronounced "greet") invited her beautiful black and white cat, Misty, to make it a four-way hugging spree. I kid you not, that cat walked over and deliberately circled the inside of our circle, rubbing her whiskers with firm affection against our ankles! Of course, when 'Guerite extended the same invitation a few days later, Misty stuck her nose in the air and pretended she didn't have the slightest idea what 'Guerite was talking about. But Misty couldn't fool us. We knew!

IRENE BURK HARRELL
Author and publisher

Encouragement means love in our family! We always remember to say thank you, good job, etc. Sometimes we do that with a special card or a phone call. I write notes to my husband and put them in his lunch bag. He writes notes for me and puts them up on the refrigerator. It's fun to find them when you least expect it!

EDIE ROSINSKI

❖ According to **Judith Martin,** the well-known writer of the "Miss Manners" column, you don't need to know a family's origins or makeup or extent to predict whether or not it will survive and thrive. Instead, you should look to the little things. For example, when someone uses up a roll of paper in the bathroom, does that person bring in a replacement roll? Pay attention to the little things you can do to show love and kindness to your family members. Small notes, making someone a lunch when it isn't expected, doing a chore for someone who is busy or tired . . . these all are simple but effective ways to care for others.

I make a special effort to send notes, especially to my in-laws, to show them how much they are loved and appreciated for all they do for me.

My son Jesse, who is six, makes things for people all the time. He's very thoughtful and sensitive and takes great pride in what he makes. Jesse seems to know when someone needs cheering up. Or he may make something just because he happens to like you. Just out of the blue he'll say, "This is for you!" It's his way of expressing love.

CYNTHIA ANDERSON

My wife and I enjoy spending time creating special or funny things for each other. For example, Jill uses blank index cards to draw or paint pictures and write verses and poems on for me. And when she wanted to learn how to drive a manual transmission car, I created a course manual called "Stick Driving 101" and taught her to drive!

PHILIP ASPEGREN

Any Day, Every Day!

We have a family full of photographers, so for years and years it has been our tradition to keep a collection of pictures on the counter in our kitchen. They are changed around as specific things happen, such as a wedding, new grandchildren, or a birthday.

We have several freestanding 4x6 plastic frames and two major turning photo holders (a sort of photo-Rolodex), which hold twenty-five pictures or more. Everyone who knows our family goes right to the kitchen to check out these pictures and to catch up on who's doing what and where. Often when we are just sitting around, we will use them for reference, from frivolous things like hairstyles to noticing all kinds of family resemblances, or deciding what flowers look good in the garden.

We also use them to keep grandchildren busy when they are eating. We show them other members of the family who live far away, or teach them the names of everyone who is coming for holiday visits. There are always a few pictures of aunts and uncles doing strange things, like water-skiing or being dressed up for Halloween.

Through the years, we have always enjoyed looking at our family history in these photos. When we replace pictures in the holders, the old ones are placed in a large brown envelope and marked "The Best Kitchen Pictures of 1991," or whatever year is appropriate. Eventually, they will go into an album for each child.

BOB AND ANN MCGRATH
Children's author,
host of "Sesame Street"

❖ Start a family "Fun Fund." Buy a special piggy bank, and agree together to put all your loose change in it. Gather together once a month to see how much has accumulated. When you have enough, plan a fun family event together.

The traditions that have been most lasting and meaningful in our family are the ones that happened "by accident"—ones that arose because our children asked for them.

One evening a few years ago, my husband shared a funny vignette he had read in a Robert Fulghum book. We all laughed until we cried. The next night our daughter said, "Daddy, aren't you going to read to us again?" Since then we have read every evening that the family is together—usually about three times a week. We have completed books by Robert Fulghum, James Herriot, Roald Dahl, Douglas Adams, Garrison Keillor, Lloyd Alexander, and—our favorite—Patrick McManus.

DONNA FLETCHER CROW
Author

We hold a monthly two-hour Copelin Council. We have a written agenda, which begins with prayer and saying five affirming things about the other. Then we move on to discuss family concerns: budgets, discipline, vacation plans, child-rearing issues, household issues, etc.

We also have a quarterly daylong Council, in which we have four hours of "business" followed by four hours of play. These have been both a marriage and a sanity saver!   DAN AND DEBORAH COPELIN

Every month, we celebrate a Month-iversary with our children. On the day of each child's birthday, we do something for that child: give a small gift, go on a picnic, go out to eat, let them have the red "You're Special" plate at dinner . . . just something nice to let each child know every month that she is really special to us.

CLIFF JOHNSON
V.P. Sales, Tyndale House Publishers

❖ Designate one night of each week as story night. Get everyone— yes, even Mom and Dad—in their pj's a little earlier that evening. Gather pillows and blankets and sit together on the floor in the family room, in front of the fireplace, or someplace cozy. Turn the lights off except for some candles. Choose short books or stories to read together.

As Fred and I were raising our family, we liked to memorize verses that were practical in everyday life. One that we used frequently to set the tone for our dinner time conversation was Ephesians 4:29, "Let no corrupt communication proceed out of your mouth, but that which is good to the use of edifying, that it may minister grace unto the hearers."

Whatever we said had to meet the test of Ephesians 4:29. Our words were to be positive, not negative. They were to build up the family members, and they were to do a favor for the recipient. As we discussed this verse and practiced using it in personal applications, we condensed it to three little words, "Is it edifying?"

Fred and I agreed with the children that they were allowed to ask us the same question. If one of us came out with a sarcastic or negative comment, one of them could ask, "Is it edifying?"

FLORENCE LITTAUER
Author and speaker

One spring I decided I had spent enough of my life laundering tablecloths and placemats. What we needed was a sturdy piece of plate glass to fit the top of our round kitchen table. I telephoned the glass place and learned they could deliver the glass that very morning. My daughter, 'Guerite, and I flew into action, looking through hundreds of snapshots of children, grandchildren, parents, grandparents, even of Allen and me when we were growing up. We arranged our choices on the table, cropping and overlapping as needed. We had barely finished covering the table when the doorbell rang. The glass had arrived and was quickly and carefully positioned on top of the pictures. Voilà! A feast for the eyes, under glass.

This table has been such an enjoyable demonstration of God's love to us that we also covered three desks and part of another desk in the same way. These are real treasure troves of what God has done—and is still doing—in the midst of us.

IRENE BURK HARRELL
Author and publisher

As our children approached the teenage years, my husband and I grew concerned about the music they were listening to. So we decided, once every two weeks, to have a family music night. Each member of the family was to bring two of their favorite songs (from different artists) for the others to listen to. If the lyrics were available, those were brought as well. We have had several interesting discussions together regarding kinds of music (our teenage son actually *likes* opera) and the meaning of certain lyrics. It's provided a non-threatening way for us to talk with our kids about something that is becoming more and more a part of their lives.   JACKIE STEVENS

❖ Stay in touch with each other by choosing one day a week, or every couple of weeks, as a Conversation Day. Do things that create an atmosphere of togetherness, in which you can talk together. For example, take walks together, go out to breakfast, go on a picnic breakfast, go for a bike ride, go fishing, etc. If you have children, let each child have a turn at choosing the activity for the day. (But be sure to explain that it must be something you can do while you talk.)

We had angels in our home when I was growing up! My mother and father always stressed that kindness was one of the most valuable gifts we could give each other. They began teaching us from an early age that it was important to care for and help each other. If one of us used up the toilet paper or soap, we were to replace it so someone else wouldn't be inconvenienced. If we got up before anyone else, we were to start setting the table for breakfast, or set out cereal boxes. If someone forgot to do one of his or her chores and we noticed it, we were to do it for that person.

For the most part, we did pretty well with this. But, every once in a while, Mother and Daddy would decide we had grown lax. So they would write all of our names down, put them in a hat, and pass it around. We each would draw a name and, for the next week, be an "angel" for the person whose name we had drawn, showing that person every kindness we could.   SARA TORTERA

❖ Prepare a special lunch to bring to a shut-in friend, neighbor, or perhaps a friend you just haven't met yet who happens to live in a nearby nursing home. Get your children involved in the preparation. They could assist you in baking some cookies or brownies, and wouldn't a homemade card be a nice thing to leave behind as a reminder of your visit? Make this a regular occurrence, if possible. Help your children to recognize how little it takes to make someone else's day absolutely unforgettable! And encourage them to share with you how they feel, too.

❖ Start a family diary. Encourage every family member to write a short paragraph in the book describing things they are thankful for or special memories from the past year. Entries can be made monthly, or more or less frequently, as you wish. Start each child as soon as he or she can write—even if it's just a few words.

My wife and I have a tradition of having a "Rainy Day Photo Session." During the year, we put the pictures we take in a box, which we keep in a certain drawer. Then, when we encounter a rainy Saturday or Sunday, we brew a pot of coffee, buy special treats from the store, then pull out our box of photos. Instead of being frustrated because we are cooped up in the house, we have a fun time sorting through pictures together and putting them in albums. And we get to relive the events we've recorded on film.   JAMES LEVINE

❖ Let cold winter evenings be the beginning of a tradition of family warmth this year. Instead of sitting around and watching TV, turn on the stereo, light a fire (if you have a fireplace), and gather together in one room. Wrap yourselves in some big, fluffy blankets, have hot chocolate with marshmallows, and spend time together. You could read to each other, talk, or play some simple games (checkers, dominoes, Yahtzee, and Chutes and Ladders are all lots of fun).

❖ Having a large family can be a mixed blessing. Sometimes with lots of children, particularly the youngest can feel forgotten or slighted as their older siblings always seem to be the center of attention, loudest in voicing their opinion, or first for everything. Take a hint from **Mark and Diane Davidner** of Kansas City, Kansas. They have six daughters ranging from eighteen to seven years old. The Davidners declare a special day for each daughter. "We don't have to do anything complicated; we can declare Mia or Jennifer or Rachel day, and just take a trip to the store," says Diane. Somehow just having your own day makes it special! And the declaration of the day can happen at any time—spontaneity being half the fun!

As a little Ohio girl visiting my Michigan grandparents almost every summer, our after-supper activities—reading, games, conversation, looking at pictures that became three-dimensional in the old stereopticon—took place at the big round dining table, always by the light of a coal-oil lamp. Except for the addition of electric lights, my family follows that tradition to this day. At night, as soon as the table is cleared and the supper dishes are in the dishwasher, my daughter and I wind down the day by playing a game together. My husband often joins in by kibitzing over the top of the evening paper. The winner for the day is duly recorded on the front-of-the-refrigerator calendar. Believe it or not, something as simple as a daily game together can provide meaningful family togetherness.

IRENE BURK HARRELL
Author and publisher

My wife and I have been concerned that the sacrament of baptism has become overlooked. So when our kids were very small, we put

their baptism days—and our own, though we had to do a little research to find them—on the calendar. We began to celebrate these dates every year. The person whose baptism is being celebrated gets to pick out a treat for dessert, and we usually talk about what it means to become a member of the Lord's family. Then we offer a short prayer of thanks. This serves to remind us five times a year (since there are five of us in our family) of our allegiance to Jesus Christ.   TIM STAFFORD
Author and speaker

"Don't Send Your Children to Church!" was the title I gave an article after a magazine publisher asked me to do so. The mail I received in response was quite negative; most people didn't read past the title. What they didn't see was that the Martys were saying, "Don't *send; bring.*" But how? Our children were growing up in a time of great discontent on the part of the young regarding the church. We knew the futility of sending, commanding, barking, sniping, beguiling, or threatening them to go.

So we started a system of making Sundays really attractive to the family. Church was a part of the attraction. We never thought of our system as a bribe. Instead, we turned the whole Sunday-Sabbath into a kind of a package deal that included going to church (which no one now wanted to miss and, admittedly, often had an alluring service), picnics, stops at museums, going to sporting events, and the like.

Not very novel, you say? Maybe not. But in our circle of friends, we found that wherever church was segregated from the other activities of the day, those other activities won out. Our tradition was to fuse all the elements of the day together. Did it work? The Spirit blows where it will, and I would not want to credit one cause or another—but it did turn out that, for all the adventurousness in their living and outlook, our children all eventually showed fidelity to the church, and to the company and events it presented.

                                                    MARTIN E. MARTY
Author and theologian

❖ Consider developing a family creed, listing what you feel are the most important credos for you and your family. For example, **Mike**

Singletary, retired professional football player, explained in his book, *Singletary on Singletary* (Thomas Nelson Publishers), that he and his wife, Kim, are working to create a strong and loving family. One tool they are using is the Singletary Family Creed, which they have their children memorize as soon as they're old enough to talk. The Creed has five points: love Jesus, love one another, obey Mommy and Daddy, pray for one another, and put family before friends.

What is important to you and your children? Make a four- or five-point list, and work to help your children not only memorize the list, but understand and apply it.

We have been fortunate to have our two oldest girls, at an early age, ask Christ into their hearts. They both initiated the process and fully understood what they were doing. Yet, we still pray that this act is seen by them as the most important thing they will ever do, and we pray that they will always remember it.

To help with this, we celebrate our girls' "spiritual birthdays," as well as their physical birthdays. We usually get a small gift for them from the Christian bookstore, and let them choose where we go out for dinner that night or what we will have for a special dinner at home. We talk about the occasion, share our memories, and pray that this tradition in our family helps reinforce the day that they gave their hearts to Jesus.

MARK AND DEBBIE JEVERT
Missionaries, Youth for Christ/USA

Especially for Singles

❖ Not everything relies on you finding another *family* with which to share activities and traditions. Around a holiday, you might invite friends over for a special potluck dinner (or prepare it all yourself if you like). Make it your personal tradition to host this dinner each year at the same time; invite whomever you like—other singles, families, seniors, children!

❖ Start a "Game Group." Find a group of six to eight friends who enjoy playing card and board games. Then gather once a month—every month at a different person's home—for games and snacks. Choose different age groups, if possible (although it's best without children due to their early bedtime hour). It's a fantastic way to get close to people and build some important relationships. These people may even become a sort of surrogate family.

✤ Since those people without family obligations have more free time—and at any hour—find a bunch of fun-loving night owls to have midnight breakfast with once a month! Meet at some local twenty-four-hour restaurant at midnight, eat and drink coffee and converse until someone is nearly asleep at the table! This is best done on a Friday night or another time when there is no work or church the next morning! (Although some people have been known to go to bed early, sleep before midnight, get up for "midnight breakfast," and then continue on with a full day, you will have to gauge this by your physical constitution!)

We have a lot of singles in our congregation who are interested in involvement in a family setting. So we started a program for families to "Adopt-A-Single" for one day or evening a month. It has worked out well for many people, and some of us have so enjoyed our new family member that we've decided our "adoptions" are permanent!

JACKSON GILLIS

✤ Singles can throw themselves birthday bashes—at home or a local restaurant or maybe an amusement park! Invite other families over to your home with one requisite—they must bring something of their traditions with them to share with you on this evening.

QUOTATIONS FOR REFLECTION

I remember my mother's prayers and they have always followed me. They have clung to me all my life. ABRAHAM LINCOLN
Sixteenth U.S. president

The Christian home is the Master's workshop where the processes of character molding are silently, lovingly, faithfully, and successfully carried on. RICHARD MONCKTON MILNES

Your first business is to take care of your husband and provide him with a little island of serenity. The second job is to tend to the children and try to make sure that they get as much out of it as they can, and give as much to it. It's always a good thing to remember, every day, how temporary this is.

LADY BIRD JOHNSON,
discussing her responsibilities
as a former First Lady

Whatever you do in your family
for your children
for your husband
for your wife
you do for Jesus.

MOTHER TERESA

See how a man treats his family, and you will see what his true feelings are about mankind.

INFORMATION MAGAZINE

Successful family living strikes me as being in many ways rather like playing chamber music. Each member of the ensemble has his own skills, his own special knack with the part he chooses to play; but the grace and strength and sweetness of the performance come from everyone's willingness to subordinate individual virtuosity and personal ambition to the requirements of balance and blend.

ANNIS DUFF

Home is the place where character is built, where sacrifices to contribute to the happiness of others are made, and where love has taken up its abode.

ELIJAH KELLOGG

A holy family, that make
Each meal a Supper of the Lord.

HENRY WADSWORTH LONGFELLOW
Poet

Families are God's primary missionary society.

LEWIS SMEDES
Author

To build a family on the love of God is the greatest thing any man can do.

ROSEY GREER
Author and former football player for NFL

[My faith] is an abiding faith—it's the undercurrent of my life. I was fortunate to be raised in a strong Christian home.

MARILYN QUAYLE
Attorney and wife of former
vice president Dan Quayle

❖ **Sheila Walsh** talked to author Jane J. Struck about, among other things, family. In an article published in *Today's Christian Woman*, Walsh said, "Fulfillment doesn't come only from our marriages, families, or careers. The only place we'll find it is in a relationship with Christ. And if every day we can be filled afresh with him, we'll become better wives, mothers, and illustrations to our community of the grace and beauty of Jesus."

My home was a close-knit spiritual family. That gave us a foundation we could stand on. When Mom read to us from the Bible, we could just see it happen. My dad always taught me to play with the hand that was dealt to me. The grass is never greener on the other side of the fence. Though he died of a brain tumor many years ago, the things he said will always be with me.

Really, family is my life. That's what it's all about.

WALTER PAYTON
Retired professional football player
(Chicago Bears)

❖ Evangelist **Juan Carlos Ortiz** wrote of his recent experience with grief in *Possibilities* magazine. "I just tested the power of faith with my family. Our son died a few days ago. It was a long agony, but because he had an encounter with God one year ago, his passing away was different. He was a positive person. When he learned he was going to die he said, 'Dad and Mom, don't worry. You also will die one day. What's the fuss about it? If the Bible is true, and I believe it is true, then we will see each other on the other side.' So he made us feel comfortable with his death."

A happy family is but an earlier heaven. SIR JOHN BOWRING

When Papa took a watch apart to repair it and put it back together again, it was a task he performed without regard to the owner's social status or wealth. He taught us that it is more important what God thinks of the job you have done than what you yourself think.

CORRIE TEN BOOM
Evangelist and author

My dear children, I am very anxious that you should know something about the history of Jesus Christ. For everybody ought to know about Him. No one ever lived, who was so good, so kind, so gentle. CHARLES DICKENS
Author

The greatest place to bring the gospel is to your own family. But until the family *sees* what you are talking about, they will never hear your words. CORRIE TEN BOOM
Evangelist and author

If we can bring prayer into the family, the family will stay together. They will love one another. Just get together for five minutes.

MOTHER TERESA

God sets the lonely in families. PSALM 68:6

To love is to receive a glimpse of heaven. KAREN SUNDE

Home is where the heart is. PLINY THE ELDER

CHAPTER FOUR

Traditions for Husbands and Wives

For this reason a man will leave his father and mother and be united to his wife, and the two will become one flesh. So they are no longer two, but one. Therefore what God has joined together, let man not separate.

MARK 10:7-9

Keep thy eyes wide open before marriage, and half-shut afterward.

BENJAMIN FRANKLIN

*T*he minute two people are married, a new family has begun. When children come along, husbands and wives can get so caught up in parenting—and in job responsibilities, mortgages, car payments, church commitments, PTA, and myriad other responsibilities—that they forget about each other. But one important factor in having a healthy family is maintaining a strong relationship between the husband and wife. Parents are more able to cope with family responsibilities when they are close to each other; children feel secure when they know their parents have a solid relationship. Don't let being a family cause you to forget you also are a couple. You married each other because you saw a special person you could love. So take some time for that person. Go away together; be alone and remind yourselves what it is that you like and love about each other. It's an investment that will pay off many times over—for you *and* for your children. ~KMB

Together Time

❖ In an interview with Rick Brunson for *Charisma* magazine, musician **Ricky Skaggs** commented:

"We really work on our marriage. We pray together. We put our kids to bed together and read to them. We shut the TV off an hour before bedtime and spend time with the kids in the Word. We lay our hands on them and bless them and pray for them.

"A marriage is also helped if the man of the house is secure about his own masculinity and serves his wife's needs.

"I help Sharon around the house. I clean the kitchen. Sometimes I cook. I change Luke's diapers. I take him so she can read the Bible and pray. I take the kids to school. True masculinity is an inward brokenness and a desire for more of God in your life."

❖ Make a list, using the letters of the alphabet, of your spouse's praiseworthy qualities. For example, *A*bility to communicate, *B*eautiful eyes, etc. Post this list where you can see it each day and focus on the things you appreciate about your spouse.

I've been blessed with what my grandmother called a "strong constitution," so I seldom get sick. But when I do, I *really* get sick. The few times this has happened, my husband treated me like I'm the most important person in the world. He brings me whatever I need, rubs my back, and sits on the edge of the bed to talk with me and find out how I'm doing, or, if I tell him I prefer it, he just leaves me alone to let me sleep. Sometimes I think his kindness and love go a lot further to make me better than any medicine the doctor could give me!
CHRISTINE HOMERTON

My mother's advice helped Dan and me when we started out. She said, "Marriage is a challenge. You can make it easier for yourself if you fall in love with someone who agrees with you on how to raise children and has the same moral values." If you share a common ground intellectually and spiritually . . . you'll have a basic compatibility. That's not to say if you don't have this . . . your marriage can't work—you'll just have to work harder.
MARILYN QUAYLE
*Attorney and wife of former
vice president Dan Quayle*

I have a sign on my desk at work that says, "Say What Is Good." This is to remind me that I need to concentrate on what is right about something rather than what is wrong. I'm learning that there is one place, especially, where this is vital: with my husband, Don. Criticism comes easily; encouragement takes work. A friend told me once that a wife's words hold great power in her husband's life. He said that when his wife encourages him and speaks kindly to him and about him, he feels as though he can take on the world. When she speaks out of anger and dissatisfaction, he feels stripped, defeated. I have made it a goal to tell Don the good I see in him—in his actions, in his words, in his attitudes—rather than harp on what I want him to change. I don't always succeed in this, but I am working at it. Because he is worth it.

KAREN BALL
Author

❖ Spend one weekend a year together, alone. No kids, no pets, no nothing. Just let it be the two of you. Go away someplace nice together. Don't fill the weekend with a lot of activities, either. Instead, walk, talk, pray, read, sleep, eat out—just use the time to relax and get rejuvenated.

My wife and I knew we would be the kind of parents who would get caught up in our children, which meant we could end up forgetting about each other. To make sure this wouldn't happen, we wrote out a list of guidelines, then posted them on the mirrors in our bathrooms. Now, every morning, we see these lists and remember that we need to care for each other as much as we need to care for our kids. Here are the guidelines we use:

1. Pay attention to each other. This means *really* listen.
2. Flirt with each other!
3. Take some time away for just us. (We make this one easier by already having a list of baby-sitters and people who will take our kids for a few days.)
4. Be thankful.
5. Play together.
6. Pray together.

LEE CAMPBELL

Sunday mornings are very special for us since we don't have to hurry off to work. We take time before church for devotions and prayer together. Bob and I share our thoughts and then pray about them. Sometimes we are in the family room with a cup of coffee, other times on our little balcony, and in the winter we are always in front of the fireplace!

EDIE ROSINSKI

To make a marriage successful, a man must learn the little things that make his wife feel special. For some, it's a special night out, a box of candy, or a poem or love note. For Debbie, it's flowers. She really likes flowers and appreciates getting them when Mark is extra busy at work, away from the family, or just because.

There's only one problem: Debbie has passed her love of flowers on to our three daughters! So Mark has started buying a single flower for them when special occasions come up. A single carnation or daisy is not very expensive, but it can really light up your wife's or daughter's day every once in a while!

MARK AND DEBBIE JEVERT
Missionaries, Youth for Christ/USA

One Saturday my wife and I had a disagreement over who should do the dishes. It wasn't that there were that many dishes—it was just that we both felt we were already doing so much that the other person should be willing to take that "unassigned" chore. After a heated discussion, we finally decided that neither one of us really understood what the other did. So that next weekend, we switched chores. I did her list, she did mine. It was an eye-opening experience! I had no idea the amount of time and trouble it took to accomplish all my wife did in one day. And she said the same about my chores. We both gained a new appreciation of the other person and all he or she does. We've decided that we will continue this "Chore Swap" at least once a year, just to remind us that we both do things that are important.

WAYNE SCHLEGEL

For the last several years, my husband has started doing something that I absolutely love. He will arrange to have several of my best friends come over on a Saturday morning for a weekend brunch. Then he and my friends' husbands will fix the food, set the table, and serve us. Not only do I get to have a good time with friends without lifting a finger, I have a blast watching our husbands wait on us!

RHONDA CROWLEY

❖ Instead of trying to come up with the perfect gift for birthdays, anniversaries, or holidays, start keeping a gift book. Throughout the year, when your spouse mentions something he or she really likes, make note of it. Mark down colors, sizes, favorite singing artists, etc. Then, when an occasion arrives that calls for a gift, you can refer to your book and know whatever you buy will be something your spouse will enjoy.

When my husband and I got engaged, we wanted to avoid taking each other for granted after we were married. After several discussions, we agreed to celebrate our anniversary every week instead of just once a year! We were married on a Monday, so every Monday we take turns doing something for each other. Our celebrations range from giving cards (funny or sentimental) or a flower, to making or buying the other person's favorite treat, to going out someplace new or fun, to candlelight dinners at home. One time my husband gave me a hand-lettered card that listed Ten Reasons I'm Glad I Married You! I still have it sitting on my bureau, and read it often.

No matter how busy life gets now, my husband and I find that this little time of celebration reminds us what is really important: our love for each other!

SHARRON MITCHELL

My wife and I found that we were becoming critical about everything, from the way people drove, to the way kids acted in stores, to each other's irritating habits. When we realized how bad we were getting, we agreed to take a vacation day one day a week from criticism. Now Wednesdays are our "No Negatives" day. If either one of us is caught (or catches him or herself) saying something negative, that person must immediately say three positive things.

Our kids have started to participate, too. Just recently I was complaining about something and my twelve-year-old son said, "Hey, you can't do that! It's Wednesday. Now you owe us three positives." We have found that this really helps us to focus on what is going right, instead of what is going wrong. MARK RASPBEARY

❖ Give each spouse a "Have It Your Way Day" once a year. On the wife's day, the husband agrees to do whatever activity the wife chooses. And vice versa for the husband's day.

Being Apart Last year I had to go on a business trip for two weeks. My husband knew I was not looking forward to being away from him and our children for that long. On the morning I was to leave, he handed me a cassette tape and our Walkman player. "Listen to this when you get on the plane," he said as he kissed me good-bye.

The tape was a carefully chosen selection of love songs and relaxing music on one side, and old radio shows, comedy routines, and songs from our kids' favorite shows on the flip side. At the end of each side was a personal message—one from Alex, and the other from the kids, telling me they missed me and were looking forward to my coming home. I enjoyed the tape so much that we started making similar tapes as gifts for friends and family who were going to be away from home, whether on a trip, for business, or for a hospital stay. It's been a wonderful way to tell those we love that we care about them. JACKIE WILSON-SMYTHE

❖ If you travel fairly frequently, consider building a "Second String" for your spouse. Talk with friends and family who are nearby, arranging for them to do things with your spouse while you are away.

QUOTATIONS FOR REFLECTION

A man ought to live so that everybody knows he is a Christian . . . and most of all, his family ought to know. **D. L. MOODY**
Evangelist

PRAYER BEFORE HIS MARRIAGE

That I may come near to her,
draw me nearer to you than to her;
that I may know her,
make me to know you more than her;
that I may love her
with the love of a perfectly whole heart,
cause me to love you more than her and most of all.

TEMPLE GAIRDNER
Missionary to Cairo

To keep your marriage brimming,
With love in the loving cup,
Whenever you're wrong, admit it,
Whenever you're right, shut up.

OGDEN NASH
Author and poet

You have to be thoughtful of each other. Don't take each other for granted. Each one should go about 85 percent of the way.

BARBARA BUSH

A family starts with a young man falling in love with a girl—no superior alternative has yet been found.   **WINSTON CHURCHILL**

When our wives encourage us and cheer us on, we are remarkably empowered.   **HAROLD MYRA**
President, Christianity Today, Inc.

In the all-important world of family relations, three words are almost as powerful as the famous "I love you." They are, "Maybe you're right."   **OREN ARNOLD**

That your Sex are Naturally Tyrannical is a Truth so thoroughly established as to admit of no dispute, but such of you as wish to be happy willingly give up the harsh title of Master for the more tender and endearing one of Friend. . . . Men of Sense in all Ages abhor those customs which treat us as only the vassals of your Sex. Regard us then as Beings placed by providence under your protection and in imitation of the Supreem [sic] Being make use of that power only for our happiness.

ABIGAIL ADAMS
In a 1776 letter to her husband, John Adams,
who was then a delegate to Continental Congress

Ronnie . . . enjoys other people, but unlike most of us, he doesn't need them for companionship. As he himself told me, he seems to need only one other person—me.

NANCY REAGAN

If I had life to live over again, I'd try to spend more time with [my wife] Alicia . . . Twenty straight years of winning football seasons, including five trips to the Super Bowl, can't begin to compare, in terms of satisfaction, to forty-two years of marriage to Alicia.

TOM LANDRY
Former NFL coach of the Dallas Cowboys

Faith in Christ is the most important of all principles in the building of a happy marriage and a successful home.

BILLY GRAHAM
Evangelist and author

Love may begin a marriage; but love does not make a marriage. You will ride a wild sea, if you think you can build your marriage upon your love. In fact, it is exactly the other way around: your love, eventually, shall be built upon your marriage.

WALTER WANGERIN, JR.
Author

From her personal journal, writing in 1840 about her husband, Prince Albert:

Ill or not, I never never spent such an evening!!! My dearest dearest dear Albert sat on a footstool by my side, & his excessive love & affection gave me the feelings of heavenly love & happiness, I never could have *hoped* to have felt before! He clasped me in his arms, and we kissed each other again and again! His beauty, his sweetness and gentleness—really, how can I ever be thankful enough to have such a *Husband!* . . . to be called by names of tenderness, I have never yet heard used to me before—was bliss beyond belief! Oh! this was the happiest day of my life! May God help me to do my duty as I ought and be worthy of such blessings!

QUEEN VICTORIA
*(from **The Oxford Book of Royal Anecdotes,**
Oxford Press, 1991).*

To be a really good lover to your spouse, you have to be a good friend.   AMY GRANT

CHAPTER FIVE

Traditions for Families with Children

Children, obey your parents in everything,
for this pleases the Lord.

COLOSSIANS 3:20

Children are our most valuable natural resource.

HERBERT HOOVER

THE RISK OF BIRTH

This is no time for a child to be born,
With the earth betrayed by war & hate
And a comet slashing the sky to warn
That time runs out & the sun burns late.
That was no time for a child to be born,
In a land in the crushing grip of Rome;
Honour & truth were trampled by scorn—
Yet here did the Saviour make his home.
When is the time for love to be born?
The inn is full on the planet earth,
And by a comet the sky is torn—
Yet Love still takes the risk of birth.

MADELEINE L'ENGLE
Author and poet

✤ To some this world may seem like no place to bring up a child. And in some respects they are right. But we take that risk anyway with the comforting knowledge that it is not for this world that we prepare them. ~KLT

Parenting You may be exhausted from working a job, or two jobs, and taking care of your children. Or you may have put your career on hold. Either way, you may wonder . . . am I really doing the right thing? Yes, you are.

Where will our country find leaders with integrity, courage, strength—all the family values—in ten, twenty, or thirty years? The answer is that you are teaching them, loving them, and raising them right now. So yes. From the bottom of my heart, I'm here to tell you that you are doing the right thing and God bless you for it.

BARBARA BUSH

My wife and I have learned to pray regularly for our children's mates, their choice of friends, their selection of a career. Standing on the Scriptures, we trust God to give his best to them and their offspring.

THOMAS B. WHITE
President of Frontline Ministries

I have kept both a memory book and a memory calendar for each of my three children since their births. I record on the calendar with a brief notation when special things happen. Then I record the event in more detail in the book. Often, I don't have time to actually write things out as they happen, so I keep a small notebook in my purse in which I jot down the event and little tidbits to remind myself of the details. Now when my children come to me with questions about their growing up and when they did special things, I have a ready resource for answering their questions, and for sparking some lovely memories.

MAVIS SMITH

If you are trying to take your children's focus off of things, be sure you are practicing what you preach. Evaluate your life and consider what you can do to simplify. For example:

1. Spend a morning as a family sorting through your closets and drawers. If there is anything in there that you haven't worn for a year—clothing and shoes—pull it out and bag it up. Then take the bags to a local shelter.

2. Turn off the TV for a night. Light lanterns or candles around the room, then play games together.

3. Make a list of things you bought over the years and never (or hardly ever) use. Exercise equipment, toys, computer games, videos, kitchen gadgets, and even books are a few of the things many people would put on their lists. Choose a charitable organization to which you would like to make a donation. Then organize a garage sale together, and give the profits to the organization you have chosen.

ALICE WILSON

❖ Make it a habit to pray with your children. It only takes a few minutes a day to do this, yet it will bring you—and your child—many benefits. For example, odds are good that you will discover what is on your child's mind as he or she prays. Even more important, your child will see you practicing your faith.

My mothering secret? I always spent time alone with each child. When they were little, we would spend at least thirty minutes a day where I had to do whatever they wanted. It seems to have worked.

DOROTHY BRIDGES,
talking about her actor sons Jeff and Beau
in an article for **Family Circle** *magazine*

❖ Have a "Parenting Checkup" at least twice a year with your spouse. Set aside several hours, or even an entire evening, for just the two of you to sit down and discuss challenges, methods, and upcoming events or issues. Let your children know what you will be doing. Give them a chance to tell you and your spouse any comments, questions, or frustrations they have with the way you have been parenting them. Assure them that you will respectfully consider whatever they tell you, and you will not get angry with them for being honest. If your children are old enough, ask them to write down what they want to share with you. Be sure to thank your children if they tell or give you something.

Each parent should spend a few minutes before the checkup,

97

making a list of what he or she thinks has been done right in the past six months, as well as a list of concerns and issues to discuss.

Here is a possible agenda for your checkup:

1. Start with a simple prayer, asking God to give you guidance, wisdom, and kindness toward one another.

2. Look at your "What We've Done Right" lists. Encourage and reassure one another that you are doing your best.

3. Consider any comments your children have given you. Address each one, considering its validity and import, then decide what—if anything—you can do to resolve the issues that have been presented.

4. Discuss the concerns and issues you have listed. Again, decide what you can do to resolve these things.

5. Finish with another simple prayer, asking God to make you the kind of parents your children need, and to make you a team that works well together. Commit your family to his care.

One of the greatest privileges in the world is to be married to my wife and to be the father of our four children. In spite of my heavy traveling schedule, one of my favorite things to do is to have creative and intimate dates with each of my children and my wife. Every moment I invest with them will reap temporal fulfillment and eternal dividends.

JOSH MCDOWELL
Author, speaker

My husband and I make it a point to let our daughter, Jackie, know that we are human, that we make mistakes, too. We let her know when we've been wrong or unfair, and we apologize to her. We do our best to treat her with the same fairness and respect we show each other. If there is one thing we want her to know, it's that we are real people who are not afraid of our weaknesses, who are growing and learning, and who are willing to say we're sorry. As a consequence, Jackie is much more willing to come to us when she is wrong and ask for forgiveness. She is learning that failures are not terrible. They are just a part of being human.

WAYNE AND KAREN STEVENS

❖ Children love to be listened to! Especially by their parents. Set aside a block of time (as long or as short as you wish) at least three times a week to listen to your children. If you're not sure what to say to get them started, ask them to tell you about the things they learned in school today. As author **Robert Fulghum** has said, "All I really need to know about how to live and what to do and how to be I learned in kindergarten. Wisdom was not at the top of the graduate-school mountain, but there in the sandpile at Sunday School." Think about it. Isn't that true? As you listen to your child, doesn't it seem that the lessons he or she is learning is just as applicable to you today? Just keep in mind that the point here is to listen!

Other topics: favorite books; friends; favorite animals; favorite Bible stories; brothers and sisters; favorite places to go; favorite games; etc.

❖ Do your best to stay in touch with your child's activities and involvements. It is easy to think you are too busy to do so, but if a president's wife can do it, so can you! In a *Good Housekeeping* article, **Betty Ford,** wife of former president Gerald Ford, remarked: "My role as a traditional mother was, I felt, very important. . . . I tried to stay abreast of [our daughter's] activities and any of the boys' activities when they were in the White House."

People protect their hearts by giving things instead of themselves. They readily give material gifts, but never give of themselves emotionally. It's too frightening to be so vulnerable. Many parents do this with their children. A number of my friends have told me that their parents never sat down with them to find out what they were like deep inside. Nor would their parents readily share about themselves. These friends had to judge their parents' love by the material things they were given, a poor substitute for true intimate love.

DICK PURNELL

We are trying to teach our little boys the joy of simple fun. [We are trying] not to overindulge them so that their happiness and security become dependent upon possessions and privileges. On Taylor's first Christmas, we bought him only one gift . . . a $5.99 stepladder from the hardware store. We knew he would be getting gifts from grandparents and friends, and we do not believe in too much of anything *except* love and acceptance and forgiveness. Amazingly, the stepladder has been his favorite thing for two years.

ANN KIEMEL ANDERSON
Author

When Chelsea was little, I had some advice from a friend . . . "Always answer every one of her questions, but don't go on like now is the moment to tell her everything you want her to know for the next thirty years. . . . [give children] only the information they want." That's true, though the first time Chelsea asked one of those [more difficult] questions when she was four or five . . . I nearly fainted.

HILLARY CLINTON

❖ If you have to travel often, here's a unique idea for letting your children know you are thinking of them, even though you can't be at home. The first time **Ann Jillian** was separated from her new son, Andy Joe (she was committed to a personal appearance), she phoned home and recorded a wake-up greeting for him on the answering machine: "Good morning, good morning," she sang in a twist on a commercial jingle. "The best to you each morning. F-O-R-M-U-L-A, formula for you."

"He loved it," Jillian said. "That's what he woke up to each morning. I figure as long as I've got to be away for three days I might as well call and put it on the answering machine so my husband can play it for him. He'll hear it and think everything's OK."

Whether you sing a made-up tune or just leave an "I love you" on your machine, your child will love having his or her very own message from Mom or Dad.

Our children love to get mail. In fact, they will fight over the junk mail just to feel as though they got something that day. Several years ago my husband decided to make use of this. He bought a bunch of fun postcards and jotted down notes of encouragement, praise, and love for the kids whenever he got a free moment. The messages were short. For example, he might tell Gavin how proud he was of his kindness to his sisters, or he'd tell Angelica how much he loved her giggle, or he'd let Cassandra know that he was proud of the way she had resolved a problem with a friend. He always ended the postcards by telling whichever child how much he loved him or her.

Just the fact that there was actually something in the mailbox with his or her name on it was a thrill. But it was even more exciting to know that their father had taken the time to send them something to say I love you. JACQUELYN CONNORS

As a salesman, my husband is on the road fairly often. Our children have grown up with this, so they usually understood. But sometimes having a dad who was gone a lot could be upsetting. So when the children were fairly young (four, six, and nine) I started having "Cheer Up" parties. I would buy a package of balloons and we'd sit in the middle of the living room, blowing them up together. Then we'd decorate the room with the balloons and streamers. I would have some inexpensive little toys wrapped up as gifts, and we would make a cake from scratch together. I'd let my husband know when the party was going to happen so that he could call home and take part in the fun. Each child got to talk with him for at least a few minutes, which seemed to be their favorite part of the festivities. The party and phone call couldn't take the place of their dad being at home, but it did help them to feel better. NELLIE STANLEY

❖ **Meredith Vieira** was a correspondent for the popular "60 Minutes" when she became pregnant. She left the top-rated TV program to ensure she could carry to term (she had experienced a number of miscarriages), and to give herself time with Benjamin, who was then a toddler. In an article in *Ladies' Home Journal* she explained, "With every day I know the decision [to leave the show] was the right one. . . . I would never be able to enjoy my [career] if I knew it was at the cost of my kids." Vieira says that she believes, if a woman can possibly swing it, that a mom's place is with her children. "I know that isn't a popular viewpoint in this day and age, but I see the impact when I take my little boy to school and pick him up.

"In comparison to motherhood, '60 Minutes' was an easy job."

Our goal as parents is to empower our children to become mature and to release them to become more independent from us and dependent on God. One of our great challenges and delights is to honor our child's uniqueness and accept what cannot be changed in him.

H. NORMAN WRIGHT
Author, marriage and family counselor

I have discovered that I honestly like my children. I like spending time with them, talking with them, being part of their lives. And I love getting hugs from them. We have made it a rule in our house that we don't let a day go by without hugging one another. It doesn't have to be a long hug, and sometimes it comes as someone is on the way out the door—but there is no substitute for that physical show of genuine affection.

TRICIA GOSSEN

❖ Every child needs to be reminded how special he or she is. A healthy self-esteem is built from the earliest age! **Mother Teresa,** the Albanian nun who won the Nobel Prize for her selfless work with hurting people in India, understood this. Perhaps you could use her words to remind your child, and yourself, of the holy heritage we have been given. Write out the following and read it out loud as a family:

> We are created in the image of God, in the image of Jesus as a human being. Every child has been created for a greater thing—to love and be loved.
> From the very beginning
> from the time there is life
> from the time there is conception
> there is the life of God—the life of the living God.
> That is why it is so wrong to destroy life—to destroy the image of God.

My wife and I began to notice that when our family did things together, our younger, outgoing daughter would get more of our attention. Our son, who was older and more quiet, often would not participate and so ended up feeling ignored or left out. To resolve this, we agreed to take turns spending time with each of the kids each week. That gave us a chance to give both of the children the kind of attention they wanted and needed. And it gave us a chance to get to know each child on an individual basis.   DICK MULBERG

❖ Remember that discipline is an important part of raising healthy children. **Shelley Fabares**, a successful actress, wife, and stepmom, was raised in a home where discipline, old-fashioned values, and the work ethic were the norm. In an interview in *Good Housekeeping* magazine, she commented, "I was a well-behaved, nice little girl . . . that discipline has served me well all my life."

Discipline

My husband and I used to spend a lot of time trying to drill the idea of helpfulness into our kids' heads. Then, one night, I asked the children if I could help any of them with their chores. They sat looking at me in amazement for a moment, then responded enthusiastically with suggestions. Since then, I offer my help every night after dinner. The kids feel like they are "in charge," giving me suggestions for how to help, and generally the chores get done much more quickly and without the whining.   TANYA ST. MARTIN

❖ If you want to be effective in disciplining your children, seek time with God. Author **Robert Cook** explains, "My authority in my home is exactly proportional to what I got fresh from God that day. I don't even have to talk about it—there's a heavenly aura when Dad's met God. When I backslide, everything at home falls apart."

   There is no better way to perfect your parenting skills than by going to the greatest Father of all and seeking his all-knowing, all-understanding guidance.

Because we love our kids, there'll always be a need to correct and instruct them. But instruction with *affirmation* is a powerful tool. . . . Start to praise your child for the things he *does* do—and more than likely, you'll find him interested in doing more. And remember, applaud effort, not perfection—for in the long run, God is patient in correcting us, even when we fail to do what we're expected to do.

JAY KESLER
President of Taylor University, host of
"Family Forum" radio broadcast,
quoted in **Today's Christian Woman** *magazine*

Responsibility

My mother always stressed to me that it was my character that counted, not my looks, clothes, or status. She enforced this lesson by putting me in charge of the pantry when I was a teenager. I was to help plan meals, keep a grocery list, check papers for sales, and even do much of the shopping (with my mother as official driver). This gave me a sense of achievement and responsibility, and taught me how much fun—and work—it can be to do a job well. Now I am married and have a son of my own, and just last year, when he turned twelve, he took over being in charge of the pantry. While I'm not too sure he is enjoying this, I do know one thing: he will learn a sense of responsibility and accountability, two vital elements for building character. And I make sure I praise him and tell him how much I appreciate the effort he is putting into his "job."

GREGORY WATKINS

My kids never used to get anything done without my getting after them time after time. Then I got the idea of posting a "Smile Chart" on our kitchen wall. Now the children earn smiley faces and other fun stickers when they complete a simple task without my hounding them. We also wrote out special activities and rewards on strips of paper, then put them into a "Good Job!" jar. When anyone gets ten stickers, they get to draw a reward out of that jar.

BARBARA VANEVELDT

I have never liked rules or responsibilities that required work. In fact, if I'd had my way about it, I would never have had to take on anything I didn't want to do. Fortunately for me, my parents didn't let me have my way.

My brothers and I each had specific chores to do. Every Saturday morning was chore day at our house. Right after breakfast, and before we could watch cartoons, we kids had to complete our list of chores. Of course, we always had the option of doing our chores before Saturday rolled around. But the rule always stood: Anything left undone was taken care of Saturday morning. I can remember whining about missing my favorite cartoon because I still had to clean my room, only to have my mother point out that it was my decision to leave things undone until the last minute.

As a result, I learned to plan ahead, to do what needed to be done without complaining, and to accept responsibility for my own actions and decisions. It wasn't an easy lesson—but I'll always be grateful that I got it. MICHELLE TRAVIS

My wife, Amy, and I wanted to teach our [now] eleven-year-old daughter, Allison, the value of money and business principles through working for her money. So at age seven, we eliminated her allowance and allowed her to choose what kind of business she would like to try. She now has a wholesale/retail pencil business, which she has funded on her own. After covering her overhead, she tithes 10 percent of her profit to Christian ministries, she saves a portion, and she gets some money to spend. At Christmas time, Allison even purchases her gifts for her family and friends out of her own money. RON BALL
Author and entrepreneur

When our daughter reached the seventh grade, she started having fits of anger and frustration. At first, we tried telling her to just "control herself." Then we talked with some friends who also had a daughter in the seventh grade, and they reminded us that this was a difficult time, physically and emotionally, for our girls. So we went home and talked with Kara. Together we devised safe ways for her to vent her anger. We bought her a beautiful cloth-covered journal for writing out her feelings when she could. And we got her one of those big inflatable punching clowns, when she needed a physical vent. That was still a difficult year for us all, but when Kara saw that we would not condemn her for her reactions to what she was feeling, it helped us all to start relating on a more honest—and calm—level. LORRAINE EMERICH

Keeping the Peace

105

My three children, ages ten, eight, and five, were about to drive me crazy with their constant bickering. Their favorite "bones of contention" were things like who got to sit in the front seat when we went anyplace in the car, who got to sit in Dad's big recliner when he wasn't home, who got to be in control of the TV remote, and so on. Finally, I had had enough. I gathered them together and told them I was hereby declaring a truce. When they started to protest, I told them that we would institute a "Royalty Day" on Saturdays. From that time on, they would rotate so that each one would have a chance to be King or Queen on a Saturday. The King or Queen of the day would get the "choice" spots, and basically be in charge. However, he or she also was responsible for helping plan meals, cleaning up afterward, feeding and letting the dog out, getting the mail, and so on. When his or her chores were done, then the final privilege came: control of the TV remote. We started this practice four years ago, and it's worked amazingly well. Revolts have been few and far between—and there is finally peace in the realm.

JANET MACGUIRE

❖ Is your child going through an especially tough time? Make a Mood Indicator to put on his bedroom door, so he can let you know how he's feeling. Purchase several beanbags, and draw simple faces on them: happy face, sad face, mad face, scared face, sick face, tired face, etc. Glue or sew a small square of velcro to the back of each beanbag, then put another slightly larger square on the door of the child's room. Put the beanbags in a box that you have covered with colorful paper, and tell your child he can pull out whichever face best suits him and put it on the door to let the rest of the family know what kind of mood he's in.

I got tired of early morning battles over breakfast with my children. So my husband and I decided to make breakfast a "Help Yourself" meal. Our children know that they can have whatever they want (as long as it's not cookies or ice cream), but that they have to fix it themselves. This has helped reduce stress for all of us during an already hectic time of day. And if my son wants to have cold leftover spaghetti for breakfast, well, I don't have to watch him eat it!

CAROLYN ANDERSON

Since we both work out of a home office, we have made it a tradition to always see our two children off to school with a hug, kiss, and promise that we'll be praying for them. Also, we always make sure that one of us is there to greet them at the door to find out how their day went.

JAMES AND LOIS WATKINS
Authors and pastors

School Days

Every fall, on the first day of school, we take pictures of our children, then place them in an album with each child's name. Along with these, we put in the school pictures taken by the school district each year. What a delight it is to look through the albums together, remembering the new beginnings and comparing heights and appearances (even the pictures where the children made silly faces) to the years before!

AMY SCOTT

Editor's note: If this sounds like a fun idea to you, but your children have already been in school for several years, don't let that stop you! It's never too late to start a project like this. Even a few years of pictures can be a lot of fun, and a good reminder of the growth that has taken place in your child's life.

When both of our children first started school, we wanted to establish a "back-to-school breakfast" tradition. On the first day of school, we got up early, dressed, and went out to a nice "sit down" restaurant to eat. We were short on cash, too, so we planned to pay for the meal on our charge card and enjoy a leisurely, meaningful breakfast with the kids.

But somehow our order took forever to arrive, and the kids began to fidget, not wanting to be late on their first day. We ended up spending money we didn't have on food we didn't eat for kids who didn't appreciate it! We learned our lesson, though. Now we drive through McDonald's on the first day of school each year. The kids enjoy the treat, we enjoy the convenience, and the kids arrive at school on time. Best of all, we can all laugh at our first disastrous "back-to-school breakfast."

GARY AND ANGELA HUNT
Authors and youth ministers

We have started giving our teens a "blessing" on the first day of school—a special verse for the year that we have chosen for each one, which we design into a computer poster so that each teen can put it on her bedroom wall. We try to choose a verse that will be an encouragement for each teen, depending on the areas of challenge for her that year.

DAVE AND NETA JACKSON
Authors

Our sons are seventeen, fifteen, and ten, and all are athletes. We have always gone as a family to every game we could possibly attend, beginning with our eldest son. Now that even our youngest is also involved, the tradition continues. The only schedule conflict that keeps the entire family from attending any one of the games is when two of the kids have a game at the same time! It's clearly a thrill for our littlest guy to have his teenage brothers at his games. They cheer for him, and he's proud to have them there, along with Mom and Dad. Unforgettable memories.

JERRY AND DIANNA JENKINS
Author; speakers

When I was a teenager, one of my favorite times of day was right after I got home. For that was when I would go into the kitchen, hop up on the counter, and tell my mother about my day while she fixed the evening meal. Sometimes I would help her with the meal preparations, other times she just wanted me to sit and talk to her. No matter what I said, Mom just listened and accepted. Because of this, I felt my mother would listen to me even if she didn't like or agree with what she was hearing. And I felt certain she would give me valuable counsel and insights. Now, after being out of my parents' home for more than fifteen years, I still love talking to my mom and telling her what has been happening. It's a great feeling to know that Mom is not only my parent, but my confidante and friend.

KAREN BALL
Author

When our teenager was going through a rough time at school, my husband turned his morning good-byes into a daily blessing, such as: "May the love of Christ be your comfort today"; "May the peace of Christ be your example today." We might never know if she recalled the blessing during the day—but we're sure she experienced God's love and our love for her flowing through her dad's blessings each morning.
DAVE AND NETA JACKSON
Authors

When our daughter, Amanda, graduated from high school, I wanted to give her a present she would always remember. So several months ahead of time I bought a blank book and passed it around to friends and family, asking them to write something to her. I told them anything was welcome: advice, memories, poetry, notes of encouragement, whatever. After it had gone the rounds, I made a list of our long-distance family and friends, addressed and stamped and numbered envelopes, then mailed it all to the first person on the list, my mother. I asked her to write in the book, then put the book and the rest of the envelopes into the envelope with a 2 on it. So it went, until the last person put the almost full book into an envelope back to me.

When I gave Amanda the book, she was amazed and grateful. And she has kept the book and tells me she reads it often. She has found smiles and counsel when it was sorely needed—and I have found a gift that will go on giving for many years. In fact, I'm already working on my son's book for his graduation in two years!
RHONDA STOLTZ

Now that three of our five children are in college, we set aside a specific time once a day for a week at the end of the summer to meet and pray with one another for the coming year's challenges. With all their jobs, etc., setting a time was hard—but we finally got a mutually satisfactory time for all of us. We gather in the master bedroom, go over the lists of what we want to pray about—take the phone off the hook!—and pray together. It is indescribable what impact this has had on all of us, for various reasons. Some life-impacting decisions were shaped by this time together.

BILL AND NANCIE CARMICHAEL
Publishers, Good Family Magazines
*(includes **Christian Parenting Today***
*and **Virtue** magazines)*

Reading

My favorite time of the day is when I come home from work and read to my children before they go to bed. No matter how many times I read them a favorite story or poem, they want to hear it again and again—and with the right voices! I have a picture sitting on my desk at work showing my oldest son and daughter when they were three and seven, sitting in my recliner with me, avidly listening as I read to them from a Bible storybook. Now that son and daughter are fourteen and eighteen, and they have begun reading those same books and poems to their younger brother and sister—ages six and nine—and to their cousins. My daughter has thanked me several times for giving her a "secret weapon" for controlling her little charges when she baby-sits. "It never fails," she told me recently. "All I have to do is take out a book, and they suddenly are crawling up on the couch with me, asking for a story. It's great!"

It's good to know that the same things I loved as a child, and that my children enjoyed and appreciated, are still touching and affecting children today. Lots of things seem to be changing nowadays. I'm glad that reading, at least, is one gift children will always cherish.

PAUL SADLER

❖ Never underestimate the power of reading to and with your children. One of the greatest authors and theologians of our time, **C. S. Lewis,** came from a home where books were considered a wonderful part of life. "There were books in the study, books in the drawing room, books in the cloakroom, books (two deep) in the great bookcase on the landing, books in a bedroom, books piled as high as my shoulders in the cistern attic, books of all kinds reflecting every transient stage of my parents' interests . . . Nothing was forbidden to me. In the seemingly endless rainy afternoons, I took volume after volume from the shelves."

Take the time to give the wondrous gift of reading to your children. It only takes minutes a day, but it may well bring you and your child great returns.

Since most of my children and grandchildren live within a hundred-yard radius of the family home, togetherness has not been as difficult as for other families! The most enjoyment comes during holidays when we gather at either our beach home or our family ranch, both being within a fifty or sixty-mile distance. During the Thanksgiving holidays we usually congregate at the ranch where we enjoy many activities. With thirteen grandchildren the excitement can be extensive including family games, hunting, horseback riding, or parlor games especially when the weather is not favorable.

During the summer months, we often go to Galveston Beach where activities are also interesting for all. Building bonfires on the beach in the evening or having cookouts are much fun. Playing games and having social gatherings with friends are always enjoyable. Ours is a close-knit family and when we are not in the family home for meetings, then the plans usually include visits to the ranch or beach.
DENTON A. COOLEY, M.D.
Heart surgeon, Texas Heart Institute

Some of the best memories of childhood can be of family vacations and planned times of fun together. Exploring new places, experiencing new adventures, relaxing and laughing—together. My personal memories of family vacations are great. I remember seeing Mount Rushmore, Old Faithful, Walt Disney World, and the Smokey Mountains. I remember fishing with my grandfather in Wisconsin, horseback riding with Dad in the Rockies, and playing with my little brother in Michigan's many parks. Each is a fond memory I store away like a treasure.

My family remembers things a little differently. You see, I was not a very good traveler as a youngster. They remember starting out every morning with Dramamine, struggling with a crabby, stubborn little girl who refused to consider this a valid vacation without at least one outing on horseback, and the unavoidable sibling squabbles over invisible territory lines in the backseat.

Sure, I remember those times, too—although I am *sure* they are exaggerating when they recall some stories! Even so, I have only pleasant memories and count these times as the times I got to know my family the best.

Discuss as a family where you would like to go. Make a list of everyone's choices, and use that as your guide for as long as the ideas last. Update the list often, since interests will change. Give children assignments, such as finding books or videos about a certain area; choosing books to read to each other in the car; making snacks (cookies, cut-up vegetables, trail mixes, etc.), or making lunches for the trip, and so on. Help everyone get involved.

Don't dismay as you pack up the kids and load up the car. I can guarantee it won't be a perfect vacation every time—but with a little work (and a horseback ride) it will be a favorite memory.

KAREN L. TORNBERG

Families do not have to be a thing of yesteryear. Warm campfire chats and sharing of emotions and thoughts can still take place in our busy lives. One of the best ways to capture these times is through the family vacation. They help to nurture the bonds of love, friendship, memories, and fun—all precious gifts God has given families to share.

FRANK B. MINIRTH, M.D.
Psychiatrist and author

On a long summer car trip, we took a list of basic vocabulary words. The kids were to learn five words a day, and every day we went over the words already learned. We didn't always manage to keep to our pace, but we did have some fun moments. And it's amazing how the words add up!

TIM STAFFORD
Author

❖ If you are trying to find ways to make your traveling more enjoyable, here are some helpful tips:

1. Have planning sessions involving everyone who is going on the trip. Be sure you get—and seriously consider—everyone's input on

where you will go. If you have a lot of different likes in your family, compromise. Choose a place where you can do lots of things.

2. Consider making family members responsible for certain things. For example, assign official map reader, hotel room checker (to be sure nothing is left behind), snack refiller (takes everyone's orders and gets goodies from machines during gas stops), toll money counter, and so on.

3. Be sure you have a well-understood and realistic budget *before* the trip. The last thing you need is to have money conflicts while you're supposed to be enjoying each other.

4. Make your vacation into a family project. Videotape your travels and gather information along the way to put together a "travelogue" scrapbook when you get home. Or go on vacation someplace where you can all take a unique class together (i.e., scuba diving, spelunking, bird-watching, etc.).

5. Pace yourselves wisely. Even the most fun-loving families need a break from constant activity. Be sure to plan quiet and rest times, as well as active times. Also, don't forget to plan some "spouse" time with just the two of you. Even if it's just an hour or so after the children are in bed, you need some time together to remember you are a couple, as well as parents.

6. Make kindness your motto. No matter what happens, make kindness the rule. Check actions and comments with the question: Is it kind? If so, go ahead and say it. If not, keep it to yourself.

A tradition we started on long trips in the car with our daughters is playing a game called "I'm thankful for . . . " We play this by starting at the beginning of the alphabet, and the youngest names something that begins with the letter *A* that she is thankful for. We then progress to our oldest daughter, then Debbie, and finally Dad. As we move through the alphabet, we usually enter into some interesting discussions on why someone was thankful for a certain thing. This tradition helps us teach 1 Thessalonians 5:18 to our girls—and it helps pass the time on those long trips in the car!

MARK AND DEBBIE JEVERT
Missionaries, Youth for Christ/USA

Anytime we went on a family vacation, whether it was to the beach or to visit my grandparents in Idaho, we started the trip with a prayer. We would sit in the car, fastened into our seat belts, and bow our heads as Dad asked God to watch over and protect us, and to give us an enjoyable trip. This simple act always made me feel safe and sheltered.

Now my husband and I carry on this tradition by praying together before going for a trip anywhere. It not only reminds me that we are in God's hands, but it reminds me how fortunate I was as a child to have parents who consistently placed us as a family in God's care.

Other vacation "traditions" included my dad singing at the top of his lungs, making up songs that made absolutely no sense whatsoever. We kids often chimed in, harmonizing (or disharmonizing, if we felt so inclined), until we all dissolved into laughter. We also played "Beaver," a game in which you scan the surrounding area for all-white horses. The first one to spot such a horse called out "Beaver!" If you were correct, you got ten points. If, however, anyone could see any spots or color on the horse, you lost five points. Other games were "Count the States," in which you tried to spot a license plate from every state, and "Alphabet," in which you went through the alphabet by spotting the appropriate letter on a license plate. The first one to Z was the winner. KAREN BALL
Author

Each year at or around Christmas our entire family checks into a hotel in a different city and explores it together. Even though our family now consists of all adults, we still carry on this tradition. It's our way of saying, "We're family." DON OSGOOD
Author

Editor's note: No need to do this only around Christmas if that time of year is already chock-full of things to do! Try another time when things are slower and you'll all be more relaxed!

❖ For a mini-vacation, swap houses for a couple of days with a friend, preferably one who lives out of town but not too far away.

Do the town. Find the local landmarks and hot-spots. And most of all, relax. Being away from your own house is relaxing in itself because you aren't reminded of all the things you "should" be doing. This is inexpensive and easy to arrange.

Following a time management seminar several years ago, I decided to get up one hour earlier to give myself a better chance to get control of my day. When my daughter caught on that I was doing this, she started getting up early, too. Now that is our quiet time together. Often we will take a stroll around the block, talking and laughing. And we will discuss what we will do with our day. Not only has it helped me better manage my routine, it has become a wonderful avenue for getting to know my little ten-year-old girl.

MATTHEW ROBERTS

Day Activities

❖ How well do you know your children? Do you know your child's favorite color, latest hero, or greatest fear? Try this simple idea to spend time with your child and get to know him or her better.

Have a "You & Me" camp out. Set up a tent in your backyard (or your living room) and camp out for a night. If you are outside, have a campfire and toast marshmallows or make S'mores (toasted marshmallows and chocolate bars sandwiched between graham crackers). Tell stories to each other, sing songs, tell jokes. At some point in the evening, play "My Favorite Things," in which you tell each other your favorite things in whatever categories you choose. Some other topics for sharing include: My Worst Day Ever, My Best Day Ever, My Favorite Birthday, My Hero (and why I like him/her), What I Like about You, etc.

We got tired of just sitting around watching TV every night, so we called a family meeting and asked for suggestions on things we could do together. Our kids came up with a pretty good list. So far we have jumped rope, had a tug of war, had a water pistol fight, gone kite flying, played board games, played tag and hide 'n' seek, thrown Frisbees, gathered balls of all shapes and sizes for a hectic game of catch, drawn pictures together, and had different kinds of races. We still end up watching TV from time to time, but now we're just as likely to forget the boob tube is even there because we're having too much fun playing together.   WENDY STAMPER

During the summer, the children and I have a monthly "Picnic Day" during the week. We pick a sunny day and head for one of our favorite parks or forest preserves. We spend the morning getting the lunch ready, and making a special dessert. We've made cupcakes, cookies, and even a pie together. Once everything is packed, we head out. After lunch, we sit on our blanket and sing songs (some favorites: "Twinkle, Twinkle, Little Star," "Old MacDonald," "How Much Is That Doggy in the Window?" "I've Been Working on the Railroad," etc.) We take along old pillowcases and have our very own sack races, then we go on a hike and gather leaves and pinecones and rocks. Everyone gets to take one souvenir home. When my husband gets home from work that night, we spread the blanket out on the living room floor and have another picnic with him, and the kids keep him laughing with stories about our day out together.   KARI WESTFIELD

❖ Not every parent is able, or chooses, to stay at home with his or her children. However, if you are a working parent, make sure you spend some time every day with each of your children. There is no investment that will pay off so well. If nothing else, schedule fifteen minutes to a half hour with each child. Talk with the child; listen; play; sing; do something the child enjoys. Just having individual time with Mom and/or Dad will help build a strong foundation of security and confidence.

Rainy days were the bane of many children's existence—but I loved them! Because on rainy days my mother would pull out her favorite cookbooks, call us children around the table, and together we would choose one fun recipe to make together. Cookies, cakes, pies, custards . . . many a wondrous dessert came from those times of making and baking together. We all took part, too, in measuring, rolling out, cutting, mixing, or decorating. To this day, nothing tastes so good as a treat I have made with someone I love!

ALLISON KYLE

One Saturday morning a month, I gathered my two children together for "Creativity Day." The activities ranged from playing with Play-Doh, to drawing, to painting, to going for a walk in the woods and gathering leaves, to going out in our backyard and trying to count the different kinds of birds we could hear singing. Whatever we did, I tried to make sure it was fun and creative. As my son and daughter grew, they teased me about my determination to stir their "creative juices." But they always took part when that once-a-month morning rolled around.

My children are in college now, but just recently my daughter came home during a break. She drove all night to get home, and I expected her to sleep in the next morning. Imagine my surprise when I came into the kitchen and found her sitting at the table, drinking coffee. And imagine how my heart felt when she smiled at me, pushed a piece of paper my way, and said, "I made up a list of 'creative juices' things that we could do this morning. So, which one looks best?" That moment—and the beautiful morning we spent together—are things I will remember for a long time.

DANIELLE CLARK

When our children were growing up, each summer we tried on a weekday, never on Sunday, to make the four-hour drive to the Eastern Shore, for a day at the beach. We wanted our children to experience the force of the waves, the tug of the tides, the joy of hunting shells and building sand castles, and the awesome feeling of gazing across the shimmering waves and marveling at this part of God's creation. Now our grown children, with families of their own, keep up this tradition. When possible, we grandparents go along, and we still enjoy it.

MILDRED WENGER

I don't know if you can call this a tradition, because it didn't happen all the time, or even every year. But it was something that always meant a lot to me. I grew up on the Pacific Coast, and we used to get some pretty windy days. Every once in a while, my father would gather my mother, me, and my sister together. He'd take us kids by the hand, and we'd all walk to the dime store on the corner, where we each got to pick out a kite. Then we would walk to the beach, where we would fly our kites until either the wind died down or it got too dark to see. To this day, my memories of watching those kites fly, and of the warmth of Daddy's hand as he held my hand while we walked, can make me smile.

ANNA KEENE

✤ Don't let your children's childhood escape you. No matter how busy you are, or how important other things may seem, nothing is as important as the time you spend with your little ones. Take time to play with them, to talk with them. You don't have to do something big. Try flying kites, reading a book, playing with blocks, taking a walk, going for ice cream, saying a simple prayer together, picking flowers, weeding the flower bed, swinging . . . whatever. Take the time to create your own activities—and memories. You won't regret it.

My parents always did simple but fun things with us when we were children. I can still remember how much fun it was to walk in the park, blow bubbles and try to catch them in our yard, have bubble gum-chewing and bubble-blowing contests, draw pictures or color together, throw a ball, make cookies, and do so many other everyday activities that seemed special because we were together. Now that I have children of my own, I have found that the gift of everyday together time is one of the best gifts I can give them. It doesn't matter to my kids what we do, so long as we do it with each other.

BENTON WRAY

Fun and Laughter   One of our traditions today is that everyone in the family, numbering twenty-three with spouses added, gathers twice a year at some Bed and Breakfast on the West Coast. There we have two days of cooking, eating, storytelling, and game-playing. Serious problems are discussed in one session, and advice is freely offered by everyone.

In another session, the financial problems of each segment of the family are discussed constructively. We believe that healthy, functioning families with good traditions create healthy children who create a healthy society.   ART LINKLETTER
Author, TV personality, and speaker

Perhaps our most productive family tradition has been our tabletime games, and the general demeanor of our dinnertime over the years. Anna and I are sure that the impact on our kids' upbringing of my irregular schedule was, for the most part, surmounted by the sheer joy, fun, and festive spirit around our dinner table. Besides the commitment to preserve the atmosphere of our dinner together, a highlight for us all has been the ceaseless parade of games we invented.

It all started with "Bible Twenty Questions" or "Bible Who Am I?" a tradition established by my father as long ago as in the 1940s. Our family expanded the games to, for example:

1. States and Capitals, or Nations and Capitals—The first person says either a state/nation/capital. The next person must complete the pairing. (We've created an impressive list of "renamed capitals," or "what the capital *should* have been." For example, it's clear the capital of Chile should be Redhot, not Santiago; Cameroon's capital should have been Kodak; etc.)

2. Share the Story—The first person starts a story (the more wild and imaginative, the better), stopping at any point, randomly. The next person must take the story line up, producing whatever he or she wants, and so on. The laughter surrounding the "weird and wonderful" developments we have come up with seemed endless.

3. Naming presidents or world leaders.

4. The List Game—develop lists from the Bible, such as, "stories in the Bible where there is water in the story," or "stories with animals," etc.   DR. JACK HAYFORD
Pastor and author

Winters in Minnesota get very long, and we usually schedule one winter weekend in which we check into a motel or hotel that has a swimming pool and hot tub. We usually manage to get a special

weekend rate, and we take along food and drinks and "picnic" in our room to keep the cost down. This helps break up the bleak January and February until spring feels closer.   Ron Klug
Author

❖ Try going on a family Green Team Walk. Have everyone carry large brown paper bags and, as you walk, pick up trash and recyclable items from the roadside and sidewalk. When you get home, make it a team effort to sort and clean your "collection" for the recycling center. If you want, have a contest to see who can gather the most of a certain kind of pop can, or who gathered the most trash, and so on. Taking these kinds of walks helps you spend time together, can spark interesting conversations about ecology and our responsibility to the Earth, and lets you do something simple yet effective about your environment.

Both my wife and I grew up in Pennsylvania in families that made homemade ice cream. Whenever friends came over in the summertime, this became a natural custom for us to begin in Illinois with our own family.

The important ingredient for us is to have a hand-cranked freezer, because then everyone gets a hand in turning. We start out with the youngest children and end with a strength contest among the older folks. We always make vanilla ice cream and spread out the toppings, including raspberries from our own garden. The moral of the story is: Those who don't crank, don't eat!

Timothy R. Botts
Author and award-winning calligrapher

Relax with your children! Laugh with them! Have fun with your family. Some of my most vivid memories of my father are of the times our family played together—swimming in the lake or at the YMCA pool after-hours (in addition to being a minister, Dad was an executive at the Y, so we could get in after hours and have the whole pool to ourselves!); watching "Star Trek" together; wrestling; having water fights (in the living room); playing croquet, racquetball, golf, or a number of other sports; telling jokes; flying kites; hiking; miniature golf; bike riding; and on and on. My dad was never a passive observer in his children's lives. He was an active, loving, vital part of our growing up. To this day, one of my favorite sounds is my dad's laughter. It reminds me how safe and secure I was as a kid, and that I was—and am—loved. My dad has taught me many things. But one of the most important has been how to laugh at life and at myself, and to find balance through humor. That is a lesson that God has used to get me through some tough times.

So go ahead, have fun. You'll be doing your children, and yourself, a favor.

KAREN BALL
Author

QUOTATIONS FOR REFLECTION

PARENTS

❖ In a *Today's Christian Woman* magazine article, interviewer Jane J. Struck quotes singer **Evie Tornquist Karlsson:** "I think motherhood has brought me closer to the Lord. With a full-time music ministry, I didn't really have a daily routine. There were some very rigid parts in my life the Lord wanted to smooth out, some practical things like what it means to maintain a home. It was a big change—but what a joy it is to care for my family's needs!"

The little world of childhood with its familiar surroundings is a model of the greater world. The more intensively the family has stamped its character upon the child, the more it will tend to feel and see its earlier miniature world again in the bigger world of adult life.

CARL JUNG
from Psychological Reflections:
A Jung Anthology

Life is a vapor. It is fleeting. One of the most significant things we feel we can instill in our children—next to a solid, deep faith in God—is the ability to be happy in the present. Happiness is something most people have to learn, for we tend to look to the past, or live for the future.

ANN KIEMEL ANDERSON
Author

A PRAYER FOR PARENTS

O Lord God, whose will it is that, next to yourself, we should hold our parents in highest honour; it is not the least of our duties to beseech your goodness towards them. Preserve, I pray, my parents and home, in the love of your religion and in health of body and mind. Grant that through me no sorrow may befall them; and finally, as they are kind to me, so may you be to them, O supreme Father of all.

DESIDERIUS ERASMUS
Dutch Renaissance scholar and theologian

I looked on child rearing not only as a work of love and duty, but as a profession that was fully as interesting and challenging as any honorable profession in the world and one that demanded the best that I could bring to it.

ROSE KENNEDY
Mother of John F. Kennedy

A parent must respect the spiritual person of his child, and approach it with reverence, for that too looks the Father in the face and has an audience with Him into which no earthly parent can enter even if he dared to desire it.

GEORGE MACDONALD
Author

Sometimes we're so concerned about giving our children what we never had growing up, we neglect to give them what we *did* have growing up.

DR. JAMES DOBSON
Author

Give me two hundred two-year-olds and I'll conquer the world.

BILL COSBY
Comedian

Parents: persons who spend half their time worrying how a child will turn out, and the rest of the time wondering when a child will turn in.

TED COOK

My greatest announcement to the world is really my kids. I think that makes or breaks what I talk about.　　CHUCK SWINDOLL
Pastor and author

Children's children are a crown to the aged, and parents are the pride of their children.　　PROVERBS 17:6

Money, status, career, power, and a thousand other pursuits may burn brightly for a time in our lives. But when winds of reflection clear away the smoke, nothing satisfies or fulfills a man more profoundly than the genuine love and praise of his children.

PAUL LEWIS
Author

A famous man is one whose children love him.　　UNKNOWN

When I approach a child, he inspires in me two sentiments: tenderness for what he is, and respect for what he may become.

LOUIS PASTEUR
French chemist

For you know that we dealt with each of you as a father deals with his own children, encouraging, comforting and urging you to live lives worthy of God, who calls you into his kingdom and glory.

1 THESSALONIANS 2:11-12

You know, once when I heard an interviewer ask George [Bush] what accomplishment he was most proud of, I wondered what would he answer? Would he say his years as a Navy pilot, a businessman, a public servant, or would he speak about some of the changes that happened since he has been president? . . . What would he answer? Well, it's the same answer George Bush always gives—that his children still come home.　　BARBARA BUSH

The reason parents no longer lead their children in the right direction is because the parents aren't going that way themselves.

FRANK MCKINNEY HUBBARD

The children again with us, & such a pleasure & interest! Bertie & Alice are the greatest friends & always playing together.—Later we [she and Prince Albert] both read to each other. . . . Oh! if I could only exactly describe our dear happy life together!

QUEEN VICTORIA
*From her personal journal,
written in 1844
(from **The Oxford Book of Royal Anecdotes,** Oxford Press, 1991).*

What I wanted most in the world was to be a good wife and mother.

NANCY REAGAN

Expressed to his father while the younger Lewis was in the hospital:
I was never before so eager to cling to every bit of our old home life and to see you.

C. S. LEWIS
Author

THE SCULPTOR

*I took a piece of plastic clay
And idly fashioned it one day,
And as my fingers pressed it, still
It bent and yielded to my will.
I came again, when days were passed,
The bit of clay was hard at last,
The form I gave it, still it bore,
But I could change that form no more.
Then I took a piece of living clay
And gently formed it, day by day,
And molded with my power and art,
A young child's soft and yielding heart.
I came again when years were gone,
No longer a child I looked upon.
But still that early impress bore,
And I could change it, nevermore.*

UNKNOWN

It is the sum total of a child's experiences that determine his destiny, including his heredity as well as his home life, his friends, his education, his church, his recreation, his job, his wife or husband, plus the books and magazines he reads, the films he sees, the television he watches. Our children are a composite of all these, some of which are beyond our control. ROBERT HASTINGS

To bring up a child in the way he should go, travel that way yourself once in a while. JOSH BILLINGS (HENRY WHEELER SHAW)
Humorist

Jeff: We call her the general. She makes it all happen—motherhood is her vocation.
    Beau: She was always wonderful. She helped you with everything.
JEFF AND BEAU BRIDGES,
*actors, talking about their mother
in an article for* **Family Circle** *magazine*

I have a dream that my four little children will one day live in a nation where they will not be judged by the color of their skin but by the content of their character. MARTIN LUTHER KING, JR.
Clergyman and civil-rights leader

My dad believed that faith in Christ had to be expressed in tangible ways. He often stopped to help a homeless man or family who was struggling to pay their bills. . . . He was convinced that if a man or his family were hungry, they needed a meal before they needed a New Testament.
    I pray that God will give me my father's eyes to see beyond the frayed outer appearance of others to their frayed hopes. And I pray that whatever I do will make my heavenly Father want to say, "That's my girl." SHEILA WALSH
*Co-host of TV's "700 Club" and singer,
quoted in* **Today's Christian Woman** *magazine*

It is a wise father that knows his own child. WILLIAM SHAKESPEARE
The Merchant of Venice

I love these little people, and it is not a slight thing when they, who are fresh from God, love us.

CHARLES DICKENS
Author

DISCIPLINE
We understand the paradox of discipline and freedom—that you're not doing a child a service in giving him no limits. If you show him what the restrictions are, he will find ways to fly absolutely free within those limits.

NOEL PAUL STOOKEY
Musician and singer

A child who is allowed to be disrespectful to his parents will not have true respect for anyone.

BILLY GRAHAM
Evangelist and author

Children learn first and best from their families. Just as by the end of the second year their language is that of the people with whom they live, so their behavior is stamped with the seal of their adult protectors.

SADIE GINSBERG

The surest way to make it hard for your children is to make it soft for them.

WESLEYAN METHODIST

A [parent] who can cope with the terrible twos can cope with anything.

JUDITH CLABES

RESPONSIBILITY
Becoming responsible adults is no longer a matter of whether children hang up their pajamas or put dirty towels in the hamper, but whether they care about themselves and others—and whether they see everyday chores as related to how we treat this planet.

EDA LESHAN
*Columnist for **Ladies' Home Journal** magazine*

Children very often are brought up believing they are guests in the home because they have nothing to do except live there.

G. BOWDEN HUNT

Every word and deed of a parent is a fiber woven into the character of a child, which ultimately determines how that child fits into the fabric of society.

DAVID WILKERSON
Author

Children have more need of models than of critics.

JOSEPH JOUBERT

SCHOOL DAYS

Apply your heart to instruction and your ears to words of knowledge.

PROVERBS 23:12

What greater work is there than training the mind and forming the habits of the young?

ST. JOHN CHRYSOSTOM
Bishop of Constantinople, circa A.D. 400

Many of the troubles of modern society are caused by broken families. Many mothers and fathers are so busy that they are never home. Children come home from school and there is no one to receive them, to pay attention to them, to encourage them if they are sad, to share their joy if they are happy.

Children long for somebody, to accept them, to love them, to praise them, to be proud of them. If they do not have this, they will go to the streets where there are plenty of people ready to accept them. The child can be lost. Much hatred and destruction is caused when a child is lost to the family.

Without the child there is no hope.

MOTHER TERESA

Most young children today, believe it or not, spend as much time watching television as they do in the schoolroom. . . . It used to be said that there were three great influences on a child: home, school, and church. Today there is a fourth great influence: [television].

NEWTON MINOW
Former chairman of the FCC

The family is the school of duties . . . founded on love.

FELIX ADLER
Educator and reformer

FUN AND LAUGHTER
Laughter is the sensation of feeling good all over, and showing it principally in one spot.   JOSH BILLINGS (HENRY WHEELER SHAW)
Humorist

Whenever you are sincerely pleased, you are nourished.

RALPH WALDO EMERSON
Author

She's incredible. She has a great sense of humor. She's my favorite person to hang out with.   CHRISTIE BRINKLEY
*Model, wife of musician Billy Joel,
talking about their seven-year-old
daughter, Alexa*

If you're not allowed to laugh in Heaven, I don't want to go there.

MARTIN LUTHER

Family jokes, though rightly cursed by strangers, are the bond that keeps most families alive.   STELLA BENSON

[Laura refuses to go to a party because she thinks Richie is sick]
    Rob: Is he in pain?
    Laura: Well, no . . .
    Rob: Then how do you know that he's sick?
    Laura: There are symptoms. . . .
    Rob: What symptoms?
    Laura: Well . . .
    Rob: Come on, tell me, I'm the boy's father.
    Laura: He's turned down his cupcake!

FROM TV'S "THE DICK VAN DYKE SHOW"

The laughter of man is the contentment of God.   JOHAN WEISS

Whoever is happy will make others happy, too.   ANNE FRANK
Dutch Jewish diarist

You have let me experience the joys of life and the exquisite pleasures of your own eternal presence.   PSALM 16:11, TLB

If a man insisted always on being serious, and never allowed himself a bit of fun and relaxation, he would go mad or become unstable without knowing it.   HERODOTUS
Fifth Century Greek historian,
"The Father of History"

CHAPTER SIX

Traditions for the Extended Family

I have a delightful inheritance.
PSALM 16:5-6

Loving relationships are a family's best protection against the
challenges of the world.
BERNIE WIEBE

Years ago, all you had to do to visit grandparents, aunts and uncles, or cousins was go down the hall to their rooms, or down the street to their houses. Now families are scattered across the States, some even across the world. Family members go years without seeing each other; some never meet face to face. As a result, the family of the nineties often seems to lack a sense of belonging or history. And we definitely are missing out on a great deal of support, encouragement, and wisdom. We need to go beyond our fractured society's resources and reclaim our extended families. We need to develop ways to get acquainted and to stay in touch. We need to regain the heritage we have lost, and remind our children that family means more than just Mom and Dad, Brother and Sister. All it will take is enough desire to do so, and a little ingenuity. Well, if you have the desire, we've got enough ingenuity to get you started!   ~KMB

Grandparents

The past puts into context who we are—where we fit. It shows us where we've come from and it shines a light on where we're going. There is security in memories, but recalling and sorting out the past is difficult for youngsters. That's why God entrusts to grandparents the special privilege of preserving and nurturing a family's understanding of who they are.

I have chosen to write a monthly birthday letter during the first year of [my nine grandchildren's] lives. I include glimpses of his or her parents' early years, words about the meaning of Baby's name, specific prayer, plus humorous anecdotes and insights. Although Grandbaby can't read these letters for a few years, they can help parents and siblings see God's goodness in everyday events.

LUCIBEL VAN ATTA
Speaker and author

I remember childhood summers I spent on my grandparents' farm in Rossville, Georgia. Each evening, we put away the day's activities, read Scripture, and prayed. I can still see my grandfather's lean body kneeling in prayer, and the worn spot on the arm of the brown chair where, night after night, he placed his hand for support.

Evening devotions spilled into the next day. After breakfast, six little grandchildren gathered on the floor and heard exciting accounts of shepherd boys and slingshots, angels with earth-moving messages, and empty tombs. Mealtimes would begin with Scripture, hymns, and blessings.

In the afternoons, my grandparents put legs to their prayers. Often I helped Grandmother and Grandfather make and deliver hot vegetable soup to sick neighbors, new mothers, and the community's poor. Often I heard them tell grocery clerks, mail carriers, and gas-station attendants about the love of Jesus Christ.

As I watched, listened to, and participated in my grandparent's devotion to Christ, I grew up loving the Lord with all my heart, soul and might. I wanted to teach my children the ways taught me by faithful grandparents.

DENISE GEORGE

We have started a tradition among our friends who are becoming grandparents. When we find out someone is going to be a grandparent, we have a grandparent(s)-to-be party. Men and women are invited, and we have a wonderful time giving gifts for the baby and mother-to-be, and showing off pictures of our own grandchildren.

IRENE PLUMBERTON

My great-grandmother started a tradition with my grandmother when Gran was around four or five. Every year, on the first day of spring, Great-gran would hand Gran a little wrapped package. Inside, nestled in tissue, would be a dainty handkerchief. Some were trimmed with lace, others had tiny printed or embroidered flowers; all were to be used on "dress-up" days. When my mom was born, Gran continued the tradition, as my mother did with me. We have not only used those beautiful heirlooms for dressing up, though. Some have been sewn together for beautiful coffee table covers; others have become arm covers on couches and chairs. However we use them, they always serve to remind us of the special women in our family.

VICKIE CLARKE

When my grandfather was still living in a nursing home seven hundred miles away, I decided to send him a postcard once every week. I figured that if I lived close by I'd want to visit him that often.

TIMOTHY R. BOTTS
Author and award winning calligrapher

I used to love visiting my grandmother during the summer, for every day we were there she would set the table with her best china and serve us tea. It was a special time as we sat there, holding our delicate cups with the utmost care, taking little bites out of our cucumber sandwiches and chewing carefully—almost as though we were getting a taste of being "grown-up."

So it was especially touching when, a few years ago, during a visit to my grandmother's house, she served me and my children tea. As I watched my little girl holding her cup "just so," I couldn't help but smile. Since that day, I have started serving my children tea from time to time. It is a tradition that is worth carrying on.

ANN GRIMES

❖ Grandparents, why not allow your grandchildren to choose an ornament from your Christmas tree, perhaps one they've shown special interest in, and take it home for their own tree? Then when they grow up and move out on their own, the ornament from Grandma and Grandpa's tree can go with them to their own homes—and someday to their children or grandchildren.

We send our son's artwork in care packages to his grandparents. We also make Grandma Calendars. Just take pictures of your child at least once a month during the different seasons and holidays. Have your child draw twelve (or more) pictures. Select twelve photographs and twelve drawings and paste those onto an inexpensive calendar you've purchased (or maybe one of the many freebies you get in the mail). Now Grandma has a personalized calendar to enjoy all year long.

DENISE ANDERSON

I mail my grandmother leaves in the fall when the colors start to change to beautiful shades of red and orange. She doesn't see the colors change in Tucson!

PAM PINCKERT

Some of the most priceless treasures you have are the ones you can lose first. In my case it was my grandparents. So this is a tradition I wish I'd started. Put together a notebook or folder for each of your grandmother's and grandfather's memories. Work with them to gather photos, cards, memories, family history, etc. Get some of it in their own handwriting if that is possible. Better yet, if you can use a video camera or audiocassette to record Grandma recalling her parents or Grandpa retelling how he first met Grandma, it will be a treasure more priceless than gold. Don't wait as long as I did.

KAREN L. TORNBERG

Three generations of our family frequently gather together to make music. We all live fairly close to each other, and so congregate at my brother's house in his living room—a huge room with a cathedral ceiling. All ages and all types of instruments are welcome, from my grandfather's mouth harp to my nephew's accordion to my daughter's flute. We have played all kinds of music—some that even sounded good! Most important, we have a great time together, and our children get a chance to get to know their extended family and to see the adults having fun and being creative.   KENT GERLACH

❖   Pass on a favorite hobby or craft to your grandchildren. **Amelia Blades'** grandmother made beautiful rag rugs. She would save up rags through the years, then braid them into long strips that she would coil into circles or ovals and stitch together. When Amelia was small, she helped her grandmother tear, braid, and coil the rags. Some of the rugs they made together adorn Amelia's home today. "And I've started saving rags, too," Amelia says. "I have some strips from [my daughter's] baby clothes and blankets, from her first dress, and from a favorite stuffed animal. All of those will one day be made into a rug for her room."

Once a week—every Sunday afternoon—my wife and I send letters to our grandparents. When we heard about our Grandma Banks walking four blocks everyday to the post office to find [her box] empty almost every time, we decided it would take very little effort on our part to make sure something is there at least once a week.
                                                                PHILIP ASPEGREN

Keeping in Touch

Making time for writing letters can be difficult with busy schedules so we give "surprise phone calls" to our loved ones when we are thinking of them.   EDIE ROSINSKI

To keep our family close together now that Bev and I live in Washington, D.C., twenty-five hundred miles from our children's homes in San Diego, we have rented a houseboat for the last eighteen years for the LaHaye Clan's Annual One-Week Water-Skiing Vacation on Lake Powell. It's expensive, but I've already warned the kids that our will begins: "Being of sound mind, we spent it all on you while we were still alive—so we could enjoy you!"
                                                TIM AND BEVERLY LAHAYE
                                                    Authors and speakers

137

My wife's family—she was one of eight children—keeps in touch by staging a three- or four-day family reunion every other year. Since people come from the four corners of North America (and a few from outside the country as well) a central location is usually selected. The family reserves a major block of the hotel, plans activities together and eats most meals together. The core of this family rests in their common faith in God. Devotions together are a scheduled part of the activities. Most family members are gifted musically, and provide entertainment and spiritual upliftment.

DAN RUNYON
Author

Because I and my sister grew up in China, where our parents were missionaries, away from any extended family members, our parents made a concerted effort to tell us about our aunts and uncles and cousins, and especially about our one grandmother. Because I am the eldest, I did get to meet a lot of the family on our first furlough. After our return to China, we would go over the pictures that were taken on our trip, and my parents would play the "Do you remember?" game. Names and events remained vivid with me, even though I was not quite four when we returned to China.

The other thing my parents did on our furloughs was try to visit all our relatives—from Arizona to Western Canada, Texas to Eastern Canada, and Maine and Massachusetts. As a result, names became faces, and we are still in touch at least once a year with many of our cousins, even after fifty-odd years.

MARY RUTH HOWES
Editor, Guideposts Books

We have always wanted our children to know their grandparents well. Unfortunately, that's not easy because both sets of grandparents live several thousand miles away from us. In addition, I know our parents feel out of touch with what is happening in our children's lives. One year when our son was five and our daughter was a year old, we decided to put together a small photo album of "A Week in the Life of Brandon and Allyson." For an entire week, we took pictures of our children as they were involved in their everyday activities: getting up in the morning, brushing their teeth, kindergarten, eating strained peas, bath time, play time, and so on. When Brandon asked what we were doing and we explained it, he drew a picture of himself for his grandparents. We included both Brandon's drawing and a picture of him as he drew it! At the front of the album, we added a schedule so our parents could know what their grand-children might be doing at any certain time during the day.

Every year since then, we have sent an album like this at least twice a year. It lets our parents feel more in touch, and it helps the children remember that they have grandparents who love them, even though they are long-distance. MARK AND ALICE ROBINSON

Editor's note: This works well for any family members who are far away. Keep this in mind for godparents who may not live nearby.

A long-standing tradition in our family was letter writing. When my mother went to China in 1925, she took with her a tradition she had started while in Bible School—writing home to her parents every Sunday afternoon. After she and Daddy married in 1929, the two of them wrote to their families, sometimes together, sometimes sepa-rately. When I was at boarding school in Chefoo, my parents wrote faithfully every week—even Daddy wrote an occasional letter. Our school had a class for the lower grades in letter writing (in the upper school, you didn't get Sunday supper unless you produced a letter written to some member of your family!), so once a week our epistles were mailed to our parents. (Strange to read a letter at fifty-seven that you wrote at seven!) Also, my mother's mother wrote to us faithfully, giving weekly news of people and the church.

When each of us girls went off to school in the U.S. (college for me, high school boarding school for my sister), we kept up the tradition and wrote home on Sunday afternoons. Now, sixty-plus years after our parents married, we still try to write once a week, usually on Sunday. Even my father, at ninety-three, writes faithfully about his activities in his retirement home and about the view from his window. MARY RUTH HOWES

❖ Sometimes it is impossible to be together with family for a special occasion like an anniversary, birthday, or holiday. Plan to be together anyway, in spirit. Set aside a particular time of day—taking into account various time zones and schedules—to do something simultaneously. It could be lighting a sparkler on the Fourth of July, reading a meaningful Bible verse or poem to celebrate an anniversary, singing "Happy Birthday" or a Christmas carol—whatever you would likely do if you were together, and whatever reminds you of the loved ones who aren't physically at your side.

Don't pick up the phone just yet. Savor the thoughts and feelings. Someone, somewhere is doing exactly the same thing you are at the same time—and that someone is thinking of you and wishes you were together, too. A silent time together—no matter how far apart—is a unique feeling of closeness people don't often share.

Now, pick up that phone, share the experience, and be sure to say how much you love them!

❖ As you concentrate on your family—husband, wife, children—don't forget the family you knew before these wonderful people came into your life. If you are carrying on a tradition from your childhood, write or call your grandparents, parents and/or siblings and let them know what you're doing and that you are grateful for the times you shared these very same experiences!

QUOTATIONS FOR REFLECTION

The happiest moments of my life have been the few which I have passed at home in the bosom of my family. THOMAS JEFFERSON
Third U.S. president

My husband and I have always valued our extended families. Both my parents and his widowed mother live near us so our children have benefited from spending time with their grandparents. We are thankful for their godly influence and prayers. FRAN SANDIN
Author

Mama Harper: "Don't allow no weirdos on the phone unless it's family." FROM TV'S "MAMA'S FAMILY"

It is the immemorial privilege of letter-writers to commit to paper things they would not say . . . to enlarge upon feelings which would be passed by unnoticed in the conversation.　　**C. S. Lewis**
Author

Home that our feet may leave, but not our hearts.　　**Anonymous**

FAMILY TIES

Family ties are precious things
Woven through the years
Of memories of togetherness . . .
Of laughter, love and tears.
Family ties are cherished things
Forged in childhood days
By love of parents, deep and true,
And sweet familiar ways.
Family ties are treasured things,
And far though we may roam,
The tender bonds with those we love
Still pull our hearts toward home.

Virginia Blanck Moore

CHAPTER SEVEN

Traditions for Difficult Times

These should learn first of all to put their religion into practice by caring for their own family . . . for this is pleasing to God.

1 Timothy 5:4

All your strength is in your union.

Henry Wadsworth Longfellow

*L*ife has a habit of taking unexpected turns. One minute everything is going as you planned, then, *wham!* Something you never imagined happens. Suddenly your world is turned upside down and nothing seems right anymore. Instead, you must wrestle with something many people come to hate: change. Even good change—a new home, a new baby—can become a difficult and taxing part of life. ❖ Some changes are especially traumatic. Loss, death, separation—these things come to us all. Fortunately, we don't have to face painful times alone. With our families beside us, encouraging us, uplifting us, we can make it through whatever comes our way. And, in the midst of upheaval, your family traditions can become a place of constancy and security. ❖ Sophocles, a philosopher, once remarked, "One word frees us of all the weight and pain of life: that word is love." The family is the one place we should be able to find love. That may not have been the case for you in your growing-up years. It is our hope that the following chapter can help you create a healthy, loving family environment today. For it is in the midst of trials that some of our closest bonds are formed and our deepest love is demonstrated. ❖ It is at these times that we can let God love us through others—and love others through us—bringing his healing touch to hearts that have been wounded. ~KMB

Creating New Traditions

The growing-up years in my family were not happy years. It has taken a long time for my brothers and sisters and me to deal with our difficult memories. However, we decided a few years ago that we would not have to face these memories alone. So we started holding "Healing Nights" together. We each keep a journal, listing the issues we are facing and how we are doing. Then, once a year, we gather at one of our homes (we rotate each year to a different house). Our families know this is a night just for my brothers and sisters and me, and they plan to do something away from the house for that night.

We start our "Healing Night" by fixing a simple meal together, then holding hands and praying before we eat. After the meal, and after we've all helped to clean up, we will gather around a table. We turn off the lights and light a few candles in the center of the table. Then we talk, sharing what we have written in our journals, sharing our memories. We only have one rule: You are there to listen with love, not give answers or excuses.

Though the memories we share often are painful, it has been a wonderful experience to talk over what happened together, to be listened to, and, at times, to have brothers and sisters gather around one another to hold and pray for each other (even though we don't all share the same faith). It is, for each of us, a step toward wholeness.

CHARLENE WILSON

Holidays were always bad times in my home when I was a kid. While all the other kids looked forward to times like Christmas, I hated it. Holidays meant a change in routine, and that meant my father would become even more abusive than normal. So I learned to stay in my room, quiet and unnoticed. When I got married, my wife (who came from a happy and healthy family) wanted us to celebrate the holidays as she and her parents had. Unfortunately, it wasn't very easy for me. After several disastrous holidays, we sat down and made a decision: We would make a list of what we really wanted from each holiday, then come up with ideas for establishing our own traditions and celebrations.

We only tackled one holiday a year for a while—that was as much as I could handle—but now we've pretty well established our own "couple" traditions for such holidays as Thanksgiving, Christmas, Valentine's Day, Mother's Day, and Father's Day. For example, over Thanksgiving, we go away for the weekend to a cabin in the woods, sometimes by ourselves, sometimes with another couple. There we take long walks and talk about those things we appreciate about each other. At night, we light a fire in the fireplace and turn off the lights, then spend the time doing something special together (such as sit on pillows on the floor and hold each other, or play checkers, or look through photo albums we've brought, etc.) At Christmas, we visit my family the week before Christmas and exchange presents. On Christmas Eve, my wife and I attend a candlelight carol sing at a local church, then go home to open one present to each other. On Christmas Day, my wife and I simply spend the day together or with close friends, playing and sharing. Above all, we have agreed that our relationship is more important than the past.

Now I find that I don't dread the holidays anymore. Sometimes, I even look forward to them! VINCENT STEWART

I grew up in a home where criticism was the name of the game. My father walked out when I was still an infant, and my mother never got over her anger at him. Unfortunately, he wasn't around for her to express her anger. But I was.

When I got married, my wife and I did a lot of talking together and with a counselor. We knew we couldn't build a family on the patterns we'd been taught (her father was an alcoholic who became verbally abusive when he drank), so we were determined to break the negative pattern within our own family unit. One way that we do this is to, every day, compliment each family member at least once a day. We make the compliments sincere and simple, and often accompany them with a hug or a kiss. The great thing is that our children, now ages four and seven, are starting to follow suit and do the same with us (and with each other once in a while!). My wife and I firmly believe doing this gives our children a sense of self-worth—and it makes us feel pretty good, too. AARON BORDNER

❖ If you grew up without a mother or father, or with a parent who was troubled and so could not serve as a healthy role model for you,

147

consider seeking out a second mother or second father. To do this, consider what characteristics you believe a healthy man or woman would have. Then observe the older people you know (e.g., in church, at work, older relatives). Ask God to guide you as you choose a person whom you respect (as a person, as a mother or father, as a wife or husband), who seems to exhibit healthy characteristics. Finally, ask that person to consider spending a few hours one day a week with you. Ask them to pray about your request, then give you a response in a set period of time (a week is good). Explain that you are seeking to spend time with someone who can help you better understand what it means to be a healthy man or woman. This can be accomplished by simply being together, doing lawn work, building things in the garage, working on cars, cooking, doing household chores . . . whatever. In the process, you will be able to talk, to ask questions, and to gain perspective and an understanding of what it is to be a healthy person.

If the person feels he or she is unable to do what you have asked, thank him or her for considering your request, then continue your search. Trust God to lead you to the person who can truly help you. When you find the person who agrees to your request, you can agree together on the details.

Or, if you are a person who was fortunate enough to grow up in a healthy and godly family, consider making yourself available in this way to a younger person. What better testimony could you give to your own parents than to pass on to another generation the values and faith they have given you?

❖ If you don't have any family traditions of your own yet, ask your friends to share theirs with you . . . or to include you in theirs. Many traditions can involve extra time, money, and work. But shared between families as a cooperative effort, new meaning can be brought to traditions and the definition of "family" can be broadened to include more than just bloodlines.

I am sorry to say that I hail from a dysfunctional family; so traditional happenings after age five almost totally ceased. [However] I do have a wonderful life and celebrate it daily with extended family members that have developed over the years. Gathering at meetings with Alcoholics Anonymous members weekly and being a part of a wonderful, caring inner healing group keeps balance and harmony in my life.

JOAN E. WHITE
Founder, Joygerms Unlimited

Moving

Just before a series of moves (as missionaries for YFC, we have moved six times in the last thirty months), we started a regular breakfast date with Dad on Fridays for my kindergarten-aged daughter. She really enjoyed leaving for school a half hour early and going to McDonald's, just she and Dad. When we moved to Wheaton, Illinois, and our daughter started first grade, one of the first things she asked was what day our special breakfast morning would be. This was already important to her, and gave her a sense of stability in an otherwise uncertain environment.

Now that our second child has started school, she also shares this special tradition with Dad before school. As the three of us enjoy our time together, we always get at least one comment from someone else in the restaurant about how special it is that the girls get to have breakfast with their dad. We think they know it, too!

MARK AND DEBBIE JEVERT
Missionaries, Youth for Christ/USA

❖ If someone is moving into your neighborhood, you can start a helpful tradition on their behalf. Make up a notebook containing the addresses of several services in the area (post office, churches, dry cleaners, hospitals, grocery stores, pharmacies, movie theaters, gas stations, schools, libraries, etc.). In addition, list the names, addresses, and phone numbers of the people on your block (ask their permission first, of course). Then, when you give this gift to your new neighbors, tell them there is one requirement. They must continue to add helpful addresses and phone numbers (their own, for example), and then they must pass the notebook on to the next new neighbors.

Because my husband is a minister, we have moved fairly often during our life together. At every new home, my husband has planted a dogwood tree. These beautiful flowering trees are Dan's way of giving something he loves to the places that have been our homes. Over the years, anytime we have gone back to visit a previous home, it has been great fun to see how the trees have grown. Last year our daughter and her family moved to another part of the state. She phoned me one day to tell me that one of the first things the children wanted to do when they reached their new home was plant a "Grandpa tree" in their backyard. So they had found a tree nursery, bought a small dogwood, and had planted it together. My husband and I both were touched and grateful that our children and grand-children have taken on this simple tradition.　　　　LUCI BAKER

We have moved three times, and each time my father went from room to room in the [new] house, asking God's blessings on the rooms and on those who lived there. After going through each room, our whole family would hold hands in a circle while Mom and Dad asked God to make our house His own, living there with and guiding us. In each of our three homes, I have felt a strong sense of God's presence and guidance. And I plan, when I have my own home, to carry on my dad's "tradition of blessing."

BRUCE SHAWCROSS

Editor's note: If you are moving soon, or have moved recently, why not have a dedication ceremony? Gather your family and friends and ask God's blessing on your home and family. Then share a simple Commu-nion service together.

When Mark, my son, was in the fifth grade, we moved to a different state. Making new friends was more difficult than Mark had thought it would be, and soon he seemed discouraged and depressed. So I started a "Cheer Up!" campaign by putting goofy notes in his lunchbox. I started out by sticking in a note that read, "Help! I'm being held captive in a bologna factory!" then continued with new parts of the story each day. After just a few days, he was back to his smiling self. And he had some new friends who had come home with him to see the mom who would write such goofy notes!

JEAN HECKMAN

Death

When my grandfather died last spring, my oldest son made a woodcut in art class of his great-grandfather and sent a print from it to each of the close relatives. What a wonderful, tangible memory of him for us all.

TIMOTHY R. BOTTS
Author and award-winning calligrapher

My sister recently lost her husband of forty years to cancer. We make an extra effort to include her in things we do. And I am trying to continue with all the traditions my sister and I have such as Christmas shopping together, etc., so she still feels loved and is reminded of her family who loves her very much.

EDIE ROSINSKI

Anytime someone I know, friend or family, experiences the death of a loved one, I write the date down in a special calendar that I keep at home. Then, when that day of that loss approaches again, I send that person a card, just to encourage him or her, to say "I'm thinking of and praying for you." This takes very little time and investment, but it seems to be a great blessing to many people.

KELLIE FRAZIERE

Editor's note: You may also want to mark down when someone you know and care about goes through a divorce or any other difficult experience. We often receive support in the midst of a trauma, but the anniversaries of these experiences can be painful as well. Reaching out on such an "anniversary" can be a true ministry to those who are hurting.

Once a lady came to me in great sorrow and told me that her daughter had lost her husband and a child. All the daughter's hatred had turned on the mother. She wouldn't even see the mother.

So I said, "Now you think a bit about the little things that your daughter liked when she was a child. Maybe flowers or a special food. Try to give her some of these things without looking for a return."

And she started doing some of these things, like putting the daughter's favorite flower on the table, or leaving a beautiful piece of cloth for her. And she did not look for a return from the daughter.

Several days later the daughter said, "Mommy, come. I love you. I want you."

It was very beautiful.

By being reminded of the joy of childhood, the daughter reconnected with her family life. She must have had a happy childhood to go back to the joy and happiness of her mother's love.

MOTHER TERESA

In memory of my cousin who died of AIDS our family made a quilt that was attached to the National AIDS Quilt in Washington, D.C.

PAM PINCKERT

Transitions

Shortly after my father turned ninety-five, he realized he could no longer live by himself in his home. When he told us of his decision to sell his home and move to a convalescent hospital, I asked him what I could do to make the transition easier for him. He asked me to gather his most valuable treasures—his memories—and preserve them for him.

At first I was stymied as to how I would do this. Then my husband suggested making a memory book for him. So I went to Dad's house and took pictures, inside and out. Then I went to Dad's neighbors, some of whom had lived near him for more than twenty years, and took some more pictures. I asked them to jot down any stories they could remember of their time as neighbors or about Dad. I was surprised, and pleased, at the response I received. I also wrote to family members, asking for pictures of Dad and Mom and stories about them. Finally, I put the whole collection together in a padded notebook that was decorated with fabric and gave it to Dad. He was thrilled. He lived at the hospital for several years, and his memory book was always right at hand.

After Dad's death, I took the memory book home with me, and it is now one of my most valuable treasures. MARGE CANFIELD

❖ When faced with a difficult time, focus on each other and meeting the needs of your family members instead of the difficulty. Talk together, ask how you can help each other—and be realistic about what you can and cannot do. Take the days—or hours—in small steps.

In an article in *People Weekly* magazine (August 17, 1992), actress **Annette Funicello** shared that, as a Catholic, she has always been religious, and that discovering she has Multiple Sclerosis reminded her that there is a higher power who "knows what He's doing. MS has brought my family closer together, if that's possible. . . . I don't know how bad my symptoms will eventually become . . . so I just take it one day at a time. And I live hopefully."

QUOTATIONS FOR REFLECTION

So often when terrible things happen in a family, one person turns inward and says, "I'm suffering so." It's very important to think about the other fellow's suffering, too.   BARBARA BUSH

We now look back and see a pattern in God's intervention in our lives. Because of Naomi's condition [chronic active hepatitis] and her visibility as a country music star . . . we've witnessed to people who might never have heard any other way. Many people now know of God's love. . . . In fact, we suspect our past experiences were just building blocks set in place by God as a platform from which we'll now launch. . . . We believe the best is yet to come.

LARRY STRICKLAND AND NAOMI JUDD
Country singer Naomi and her husband,
*quoted in **Charisma** magazine*

Trouble is a part of your life, and if you don't share it, you don't give the person who loves you enough chance to love you enough.

DINAH SHORE
Singer

[When things are really rough], I urge people to seek out somebody they can talk to. That's real important. Sometimes professionals are the best. Sometimes ministers or priests or friends or relatives. [Find] somebody.   HILLARY CLINTON

Jarrod Barkley: "Whatever trouble he's in, his family has the right to share it with him. It's our duty to help him if we can and it's his duty to let us and he doesn't have the privilege to change that."
FROM TV'S "THE BIG VALLEY"

I have always grown from my problems and challenges, from the things that don't work out—that's when I've really learned.
CAROL BURNETT
Comedienne

I the Lord do not change.   MALACHI 3:6

The only thing in life that never changes is change.   ANONYMOUS

More than time is required to heal a badly broken family. It takes meaningful actions and knowing how to say "I love you."
GRAHAM KERR
Gourmet cook and author

CHAPTER EIGHT

The Joy of Family

I will open my mouth in parables, I will utter hidden things, things from of old—what we have heard and known, what our fathers have told us. We will not hide them from their children; we will tell the next generation the praiseworthy deeds of the Lord, his power, and the wonders he has done.

PSALM 78:2-4

It is a reverent thing to see an ancient castle or building not in decay: or to see a fair timber tree sound and perfect. How much more to behold an ancient and noble family which hath stood against the waves and weathers of time.

SIR FRANCIS BACON

Hear this, you elders;

listen, all who live in the land.

Has anything like this ever happened in your days

or in the days of your forefathers?

Tell it to your children,

and let your children tell it to their children,

and their children to the next generation."   JOEL 1:2-3

✤ When the prophet Joel first said this, he was referring to an invasion of locusts! But the words carry good advice in any circumstances. As we live our lives we experience and learn a lot. Don't let any of that go to waste. Your children and grandchildren can benefit many times over as they hear about the history of their family. They can learn from your successes *and* your failures. ✤ And as they hear stories about their family that go back several generations, they will gain an awesome view of their own lives and the impact *they* can have on generations to come. ✤ Tell those stories, carry on those traditions, invest in the future. ~KLT

A family is literally a "museum of memories." **DR. JAMES DOBSON**
Straight Talk to Men and Their Wives

What greater thing is there for human souls than to feel that they are joined for life—to strengthen each other in all labor, to rest on each other in all sorrow, to minister to each other in all pain, and to be with each other in silent unspeakable memories.

GEORGE ELIOT
English novelist

❖ In a *Newsweek* article, **Ellen J. Miller** spoke of her mother, who was born in Berlin in 1902 and fled to Holland with her father when Hitler came to power in 1933. The family members who stayed behind died in the Holocaust.

"Years ago my mother and I sat talking at my kitchen table while a portable recorder taped our conversation. I had decided to make an oral history of our family while there was still time and memory. . . . I asked my mother about her everyday life—what was her school day like, who were her friends, was there enough to eat during World War I? . . . My mother's memories tumbled out and the tape rolled on. . . . My mother was eighty-eight when she died recently. . . . I edited the tape recording into a twelve-minute videotape that blended family photographs, my own narration, and my mother's favorite Beethoven piano sonata."

Traditions and rituals give importance to a moment, a sense of grace. They allow us to acknowledge an important moment or change in our lives.

JAY O'CALLAHAN
Author

A family is a link to the past, a bridge to the future. **ALEX HALEY**
Author

❖ Have a "Family Tradition" night. Gather your family together and have each person complete this sentence: "The family tradition I like best is . . . ." If you can't think of any traditions, or if you only have a few, discuss what new traditions you would like to start in the next year. **Dr. Paul Pearsall** says studies show that families that celebrate traditions together are happier than families that do not. He advocates taking your commitment to traditions rather seriously and "making time for your shared rituals." Dr. Pearsall says these traditions promote a feeling of "us"—and that feeling of connection is important to good mental health.

Make your family's mental health a priority this year. Start celebrating!

The family you come from isn't as important as the family you're going to have.
Ring Lardner

❖ Start a notebook of how God has worked in the life of your family. Go back as far as you can remember, even to stories told to you by your parents and grandparents. This will serve as the "spiritual history" of your family, and is something you should bring out to read and discuss often with your children.

Because of our traditions, every one of us knows who he is, and what God expects of him.
Tevye, from *Fiddler on the Roof*

If you have a family memory or tradition that you would like to share, or a suggestion for a tradition, we would love to hear from you! Send it with your name and address to:

Family Traditions
c/o Tyndale House Publishers, Inc.
P.O. Box 80
Wheaton, Illinois 60189-0080
attn: Karen Ball

Index of contributors and sources

Imaginative, Practical Resources for Home and Family— from Tyndale House

THE BIG BOOK OF GREAT GIFT IDEAS
0-8423-1148-3
GREAT CHRISTMAS IDEAS
0-8423-1056-8
Alice Chapin
Hundreds of creative, inexpensive ideas for gift-giving and ways to recapture the meaning of Christmas.

FAMILY DEVOTIONS FOR THE ADVENT SEASON
James Evans   0-8423-0865-2
Contains a devotional and family activity for each day of Advent.

THE ONE YEAR BIBLE MEMORY BOOK FOR FAMILIES
David R. Veerman   0-8423-1387-7
Weekly Bible verses and application notes in a page-a-day format help families memorize Scripture together.

THE WELCOMING HEARTH
Elizabeth R. Skoglund   0-8423-7919-3
Discover the often neglected spiritual gift of hospitality and turn your home into a place of comfort and ministry.

THE FAMILY DEVOTIONS BIBLE
This fantastic Bible teaches key biblical values through easy-to-use devotionals, positioned right next to the Scriptures on which they are based. Available in *The Living Bible* version, hardcover and softcover.